English Olympiad

Highly useful for all school students participating in Various Olympiads & Competitions

Series Editor Keshav Mohan
Author Gajendra Singh

Class 8

arihant

ARIHANT PRAKASHAN, MEERUT

ARIHANT PRAKASHAN, MEERUT

All Rights Reserved

卐 **© Publisher**

卐 **Administrative & Production Offices**

Regd. Office   'Ramchhaya' 4577/15, Agarwal Road, Darya Ganj New Delhi -110002
Tele: 011- 47630600, 43518550; Fax: 011- 23280316

Head Office   Kalindi, TP Nagar, Meerut (UP) - 250002
Tele: 0121-2401479, 2512970, 4004199; Fax: 0121-2401648

All disputes subject to Meerut (UP) jurisdiction only.

卐 **Sales & Support Offices**

Agra, Ahmedabad, Bengaluru, Bhubaneswar, Bareilly, Chennai, Delhi, Guwahati, Haldwani, Hyderabad, Jaipur, Jhansi, Kolkata, Kota, Lucknow, Meerut, Nagpur & Pune

卐 **ISBN**   978-93-5203-405-5

卐 **Price**   ₹80.00

Typeset by Arihant DTP Unit at Meerut
Printed & Bound by Arihant Publications (I) Ltd. (Press Unit)

Production Team

Publishing Manager	Mahendra Singh Rawat	*Page Layouting*	Diwakar Gaur
Project Head	Karishma Yadav	*DTP Operator*	Vinay Sharma
Project Coordinator	Divya Gusain	*Cover Designer*	Syed Darin Zaidi
Proof Reader	Megha Tiwari & Chetna Sharma	*Inner Designer*	Deepak Kumar

For further information about the products from Arihant
log on to www.arihantbooks.com or email to info@arihantbooks.com

Preface

English Olympiad Series for Class 6th -10th is a series of books which will challenge the young inquisitive minds by the non-routine and exciting Questions on the use of English.

The main purpose of this series is to make the students ready for competitive exams, as English Language is an integral section of almost all competitive examinations. All the questions given in this series are objective in nature so they will provide students a feel of competitive examinations as school/board exams are of qualifying nature but not competitive, which mainly have objective questions.

- **Need of Olympiad Series**
  This series helps students who are willing to sharpen their proficiency in the field of English language. Unlike typical assessment books, which emphasise on drilling practice, the focus of this series is on practising problem solving techniques. It will help the students use the concepts they have learnt to discover that they can actually solve questions.

- **Development of Communication Skills**
  Application based questions given in this series will help students to attain a deeper understanding of different concepts of English Language through which students will be able to imbibe more effective communication skills in themselves.

- **Complement Your School Studies**
  This series complements the additional preparation needs of students for regular school/board exams. By learning English effectively, students will not only be able to perform well in English language exam but also they will perform better in Science/Social Science/Mathematics where medium to write the answer is English. Along with, it will also address all the requirements of the students who are approaching National/State level competitions or Olympiads.

We shall welcome criticism from the students, teachers, educators and parents. We shall also like to hear from all of you about errors and shortcomings which may have remained in this edition and the suggestions for their improvement in the next edition.

Editor & Author

Contents

1 Active and Passive Voice

There are two ways to express an action of a subject in relation to its object
- Active voice – the subject acts upon the object
- Passive voice – the object is acted upon by the subject

The normal structure of an active voice sentence is **subject + verb + object** but in passive voice the normal structure of the sentence is reversed according to certain rules and becomes **object + verb + subject**.

The real meaning of a sentence does not change if the sentence is expressed either by active voice or by passive voice.

Rules for Changing a Sentence

The fundamental rules for changing a sentence from active voice to passive voice are

Rule 1 The places of subject and object are interchanged, i.e. the object shifts to the place of the subject and the subject shifts to the place of the object in passive voice.

Example
Active voice: I write a letter.
Passive voice: A letter is written by me.

Subject (I) of the sentence has been shifted to the place of the object (letter) and the object (letter) has been shifted to the place of subject (I) in passive voice.

Rule 2 Sometimes the subject of the sentence is not used in passive voice. Subject of the sentence can be omitted in passive voice, if without subject it can give enough meaning in passive voice.

Example
Passive voice: Cloth is sold in metres.

Rule 3 Third form of the verb (past participle) is always used as main verb in sentences of passive voice for all tenses. The base form of the verb or present participle will be never used in passive voice. In addition, the words *by, with* or *to* (depending on the context) are used before the subject in sentences in passive voice.

Example
(a) *Active voice:* He sings a song.   *Passive voice:* A song is sung by him.
(b) *Active voice:* Water fills the tub.   *Passive voice:* The tub is filled with water.
(c) *Active voice:* He knows me.   *Passive voice:* I am known to him.

Rule 4 Auxiliary verbs are used in passive voice according to the tense of the sentence of its active voice form.

Example
(a) *Active voice:* I am writing a letter. *Passive voice:* A letter is being written by me.
(b) *Active voice:* I did not kill a snake. *Passive voice:* A snake was not killed by me.
(c) *Active voice:* She will buy a car.   *Passive voice:* A car will be bought by her.

Practice Centre

Exercise I

Change the given sentences using the passive voice and keeping the same tense as given in the example. Choose from the given options.

> **Example :** They closed this shop at 5 o'clock.
>
>   a This shop is being closed at 5 o'clock.
>   b This shop was closed at 5 o'clock.
>   c The shop has been closed at 5 o'clock.
>   d This shop will be closed at 5 o'clock.
>
> **Ans. (b)**

1. They make these tractors in Germany.
   a These tractors are being made in Germany.
   b These tractors are made in Germany.
   c These tractors were made in Germany.
   d These tractors have been made in Germany.

2. You must not drop garbage on the road.
   a Garbage must not be dropped on the road.
   b Garbage is not to be dropped on the road.
   c Garbage will not be dropped on the road.
   d Garbage is not supposed to be dropped on the road.

3. Someone broke my bedroom window last night.
   a My bedroom window was broken last night.
   b My bedroom window had been broken last night.
   c My bedroom window was being broken last night.
   d My bedroom window has been broken last night.

4. The mechanic has already repaired the TV set.
   a The TV set has already been repaired by the mechanic.
   b The TV set was already been repaired by the mechanic.
   c The TV set will have already been repaired by the mechanic.
   d The TV set had already been repaired by the mechanic.

5. People will need public transport.
   a Public transport is needed.
   b Public transport was needed.
   c Public transport will be needed by people.
   d Public transport would be needed.

6. The workmen are plastering the wall.
   a The wall is being plastered by the workmen.
   b The wall was been plastered.
   c The wall has been plastered.
   d The wall is getting plastered.

7. You should not replace the sofa set.
   a The sofa set is not to be replaced.
   b The sofa set should not be replaced.
   c The sofa set will not be replaced.
   d The sofa set should not be getting replaced.

8. People are spending more money this year on food.
   a More money will be spent this year on food.
   b More money was being spent this year on food.
   c More money is being spent this year on food by people.
   d More money has been spent this year on food.

9. People speak Portuguese in Brazil.
   a Portuguese is spoken in Brazil.
   b Portuguese is being spoken in Brazil.
   c Portuguese was spoken in Brazil.
   d Portuguese has been spoken in Brazil.

10. Somebody must have stolen my purse.
   a My purse is being stolen.
   b My purse must have been stolen.
   c My purse was stolen.
   d My purse may have been stolen.

Exercise II

Fill in the blanks with suitable active or passive verb forms using the correct options.

1. This house _____ in 1970 by my grandmother.
   a built   b was built
   c were built   d has built

2. The robbers _____ by the police.
   a have arrested   b have been arrested
   c was arrested   d had arrested

3. We _____ for the examinations.
   a have preparing   b are preparing
   c had preparing   d has been preparing

4. It _____ since yesterday.
   a is raining
   b has been raining
   c have been raining
   d will be raining

5. The students _____ to submit their reports by the end of this week.
   a have been asked
   b are asked
   c has asked
   d are asking

6. She _____ for a while.
   a are ailing   b is been ailing
   c has been ailing   d have been ailing

7. The students _____ by the teacher for stealing in the class.
   a has been punished b were being punished
   c were been punished d are punished

8. As the patient could not walk, he _____ home in a wheel chair.
   a has carried   b has being carried
   c was carried   d was carrying

9. The injured _____ to the hospital.
   a were taking   b was taking
   c were taken   d have taken

10. The inmates of the juvenile home _____ well by their caretakers.
   a were not being treated
   b were not treating
   c have not being treated
   d was not being treated

Exercise III

In the story (Bank Robbery) given below, fill in the blanks by choosing the correct options with the correct form of the verbs

The police **1.**_________ just **2.**_________ that the local State Bank **3.**_________ yesterday. Two men **4.**_________ the bank at 12 noon with guns in their hands. Customers and bank clerks **5.**_________ to lie down on the floor and one of the bank clerks **6.**_________ to fill the robbers' bags with money. After that the two men **7.**_________ the bank quickly. The police Inspector Karan Saxena says that more than Rupees 4 crores **8.**_________ yesterday, but nobody **9.**_________ . Karan Saxena believes that the robbers **10.**_________ soon. The bank **11.**_________ since yesterday.

1.	a have	b had	c has	d will have
2.	a been announced	b announced	c have announced	d being announced
3.	a had been robbed	b has been robbed	c was robbed	d was being robbed
4.	a entered	b had entered	c was entered	d enter
5.	a was asked	b were asked	c were being asked	d were ask
6.	a was made	b was being made	c has been made	d had been made
7.	a had left	b left	c has left	d leave
8.	a had been robbed	b were robbed	c have been robbed	d has been robbed
9.	a was injured	b injured	c has been injured	d had been injured
10.	a are found	b will be found	c has been found	d would be found
11.	a are closed	b will be closed	c has been closed	d had been closed

Exercise IV

In this exercise, the first sentence is in the active voice. Choose the most correct way of saying the same thing in the passive form from the given options.

1. They were interviewing her for the job.
   She _____ for the job.
   - a was being interviewed
   - b was interviewed
   - c has been interviewed
   - d been interviewed

2. Tom is writing the letter.
   The letter _____ by Tom.
   - a is written
   - b is being written
   - c was written
   - d was being written

3. Everyone understands English.
   English _____ by everyone.
   - a was understood
   - b has been understood
   - c is understood
   - d is understand

4. The employees brought up this issue during the meeting.
   This issue _____ by the employees during the meeting.
   - a has been brought up
   - b is brought up
   - c was brought up
   - d had been brought up

5. The professor told him not to talk in class.
   He _____ by the professor not to talk in the class.
   - a was told
   - b was being told
   - c has been told
   - d had been told

6. They say that women are smarter than men.
   Women _____ to be smarter than men.
   - a were being said
   - b are said
   - c were said
   - d had been said

7. She would have told you about the deal.
   You _____ by her about the deal.
   - a would have been told
   - b would be told
   - c were being told
   - d will have been told

8. The fire has destroyed the house.
   The house _____ by the fire.
   - a was being destroyed
   - b is destroyed
   - c has been destroyed
   - d was been destroyed

9. She will reject this offer.
   This offer _____ rejected by her.
   - a will be
   - b has been
   - c is being
   - d would be

Exercise V

Complete the questions in passive voice by filling in the blanks in the conversation given below. Choose from the given options.

Salim There was a storm on the coast last night.

Saira **1.** _____?

Salim Yes, some trees fell on cars. Fortunately, nobody was killed.

Saira How many cars **2.** _____ during the storm?

Salim Three or four.

Saira **3.** _____?

Salim Yes, they have. But the cars are still there.

Saira When **4.** _____ ?

Salim Tomorrow, I hope.

Saira **5.** _____?

Salim Yes, they are. One of them is completely destroyed.

1.
   - a Is anything damaged by the storm
   - b Was anything damaged by the storm
   - c Has anything being damaged by the storm
   - d Had anything been damaged by the storm

2.
   - a had been crushed
   - b were crushed
   - c are crushed
   - d has been crushed

3.
   - a Had the trees been removed yet
   - b Are the trees been removed yet
   - c Have the trees been removed yet
   - d Were the trees removed yet

4.
   - a will the cars be removed
   - b are the cars been removed
   - c were the cars removed
   - d will the cars being removed

5.
   - a Are the cars badly damaged
   - b Have the cars been badly damaged
   - c Were the cars been badly damaged
   - d Had the cars been badly damaged

2 *Punctuation*

A punctuation mark is a mark such as a full stop, comma, question mark, etc., used in writing to separate sentences and their elements and to clarify meaning. Capitalisation of letters is also included under the topic of punctuation.

Punctuation marks used in English along with their rules and examples are given below

Punctuation Mark	Use	Example
Capitalisation of letters	• Always start a sentence with a capital letter. • Use capital letters to start proper nouns like names and titles. • Use capital letters for acronyms. An acronym is a word formed from the first letter of every word in a long proper noun or title.	• He had high fever. • Her Majesty, Mr President, etc. • CBI, BSF, etc.
(.) Period	• End a sentence.	• The food was delicious.
(?) Question Mark	• End a sentence and denote enquiry.	• What time is it?
(!) Exclamation Mark	• End a sentence and denote excitement or emphasis.	• Watch out for that truck!
(,) Comma	• Indicate a break or pause within a sentence. • When listing items in a series. • To separate two or more adjectives describing a noun. • Separate one geographical area from another that is located inside it. • Separate an introductory phrase from the rest of the sentence. • Separate two independent clauses in a sentence. • Make a direct address. • Separate direct quotes from the part of the sentence introducing them.	• Malvika, listen to me. • Please buy eggs, milk, butter and bread. • He is a charming, attentive listener. • I live in Rewari, Haryana. • After the show, Ashok and I went out to dinner. • The waiter still hasn't taken our order, and the play starts in five minutes. • Arvind, could you come here for a moment? • Said the teacher, "Silence in the class."
(;) Semicolon	• To separate closely related independent clauses.	• My father never goes to bed early; he's afraid to miss his favourite TV serial.
(:) Colon	• Introduce a list. • Introduce a new concept or example. • Introduce a statement that expands upon the clause before the colon.	• For Diwali, I want the following presents: a video game, a mobile phone and a cricket bat. • There's only one person old enough to remember that wedding: grandma. • And so, my fellow countrymen: ask not what your country can do for you-ask what you can do for your country.
(-) Hyphen	• Adding a prefix to some words. • Creating compound words from several smaller words. • Writing numbers out as words.	• Trans-Atlantic flights are costly. • Spider-Man is my favorite superhero. • I have lived in this house for thirty-three years.
(– or –) Dash	• Making a brief interruption within a statement.	• Salim asked me–with a straight face, I might add–if he could borrow my bike for the day.
(") Quotation	• To enclose a direct quotation, whether spoken by a person or taken from a written source.	• "If you pick up a starving dog and make him prosperous, he will not bite you."
(') Apostrophe	• Together with the letter s to indicate possession. • To combine two words to make a contraction.	• I believe that is Allen's pen. • I know it's his because of the distinct monogram.
(( )) Parentheses	• To clarify. • Indicate an afterthought or personal commentary.	• Please bring home some real butter (as opposed to margarine). • Anyone can edit Wikipedia (not that there's anything wrong with that).

Practice Centre

Exercise I

Select the correctly punctuated sentence from the given options.

1.   a   My three favourite foods are pasta, pizza, and ice-cream.
      b   My three favourite foods are pasta, pizza and ice-cream.
      c   My three favourite foods, are pasta pizza and ice-cream.

2.   a   I like to run, but not when it's hot.
      b   I like to run but not when it's hot.
      c   I like, to run but not when it's hot.

3.   a   When I go to the mall I will go to the food court.
      b   When I go, to the mall; I will go to the food court.
      c   When I go to the mall, I will go to the food court.

4.   a   Tomorrow, Wednesday, we will take a trip to the zoo.
      b   Tomorrow, Wednesday we will take a trip to the zoo.
      c   Tomorrow Wednesday we will take a trip to the zoo.

5.   a   ''Gas is too expensive'' said the experienced driver.
      b   ''Gas is too expensive'', said the experienced driver.
      c   Gas is too expensive said the experienced driver.

6.   a   Yes we can find a place for you to stay over the weekend.
      b   Yes, we can find a place for you to stay over the weekend.
      c   yes we can, find a place, for you to stay over the weekend.

7.   a   Today is Tuesday June 10th 1992.
      b   Today, is Tuesday June 10th, 1992
      c   Today is Tuesday, June 10th, 1992.

8.   a   I need to call Sally, Tom Brad, and Keshu about the party
      b   I need to call Sally, Tom Brad and Keshu, about the party.
      c   I need to call Sally, Tom Brad and Keshu about the party.

Exercise II

Select the correctly punctuated sentence from the given options.

1.   a   The children's books were all left in the following places: Mr Smith's room, Mr Powell's office and the caretaker's cupboard.
      b   The children's books were all left in the following places; Mrs Smith's room, Mr Powell's office and the caretaker's cupboard.
      c   The childrens books were all left in the following places : Mrs Smiths room, Mr Powells office and the caretakers cupboard.

2.   a   She always enjoyed: Sweets, chocolate marshmallows and toffee apples.
      b   She always enjoyed Sweet's, chocolates, marshmallow's and toffee apple's.
      c   She always enjoyed sweets, chocolates, marshmallows and toffee apples.

3.   a   Shobha's mummy's car was found without its wheels in that old derelict warehouse.
      b   Shobha's mummy's car was found without its wheels in that old, derelict warehouse.
      c   Shobha's mummy's car was found without it's wheels in that old derelict warehouse.

4.   a   I cant see Mudit's car; there must have been, an accident.
      b   I can't see Mudit's car there must have been an accident.
      c   I can't see Mudit's car; there must have been an accident.

5.   a   Pooja's aunty was terrible, so her brother's friends went round to have a word with her.
      b   Pooja's aunty was terrible; So her brother's friends went round to have a word.
      c   Pooja's aunty was terrible so her brothers' friends went round to have a word with her.

6.   a   Geetika's granny, a formidable woman, always bought her chocolates, cakes sweets and a nice fresh apple.
      b   Geetikas granny a formidable woman always bought her chocolates, cakes, sweets and a nice fresh apple.
      c   Geetika's granny, a formidable woman, always bought her chocolates, cakes, sweets and a nice fresh apple.

7.   a   We decided to visit: Spain, Greece, Portugal and Italy's mountains.
      b   We decided to visit Spain, Greece, Portugal and Italys mountains.
      c   We decided to visit Spain, Greece, Portugal and Italy's mountains.

ENGLISH OLYMPIAD CLASS VIII

Exercise III

Write the following sentences with appropriate capital letters and punctuation. Choose from the given options.

1. my favourite books are green eggs and ham and horton hears a who both by dr seuss.
   a My favourite books are "Green Eggs and Ham" and "Horton Hears a Who!", both by Dr Seuss.
   b My Favourite books are "Green Eggs and Ham" and "Horton Hears a who", both by Dr Seuss.
   c My favourite Books are "Green Eggs and Ham" and "Horton Hears a who", both by Dr Seuss.

2. on sunday i will see the movie star wars and eat at Munch restaurant.
   a On Sunday, I will see the movie Star wars and eat at 'munch' restaurant.
   b On Sunday, I will see the movie "Star Wars" and eat at Munch restaurant.
   c on sunday I will see the movie star-wars and eat at Munch restaurant.

3. the best television shows are spongebob and ed, chota bheem and pogo.
   a The best television shows are spongebob and Ed, Chota bheem and Pogo.
   b The best Television shows are Spongebob and Ed, Chota Bheem and Pogo.
   c The best television shows are—Spongebob and Ed, Chota Bheem and Pogo.

4. julius caesar, the roman general was Born about, 100 bc
   a Julius caesar the Roman general was born about 100 b.c.
   b Julius Caesar, the Roman general, was born about 100 B.C.
   c Julius Caesar, the Roman General, was born about 100 b.c.

5. moms list included the following Milk, Eggs, butter, Tooth paste and, Soap.
   a mom's list included the following milk, eggs butter, toothpaste and soap.
   b Mom's list included the following milk, eggs, butter, toothpaste and soap.
   c Mom's list included the following: milk, eggs, butter, toothpaste and soap.

6. shelly one of the greatest english poets was also a fine playwright
   a Shelly, one of the greatest english poets, was also a fine playwright.
   b Shelly, one of the greatest English poets, was also a fine playwright.
   c Shelly, one of the greatest English poets, was also a fine Playwright.

Exercise IV

Which choice correctly punctuates and capitalises the following sentences?

1. a St Patricks day comes once a year.
   b St Patrick's Day comes once a year.
   c St Patricks Day comes once a year.

2. a You must go 10 miles north to get to edinburgh.
   b You must go 10 miles North to get to edinburgh.
   c You must go 10 miles North to get to Edinburgh.

3. a You're going to come to my party, right?
   b Youre going to come to my party right.
   c You're going to come to my party, right.

4. a In addition to putting your name on your paper please add the date.
   b In addition to putting your name on your paper, please add the date.
   c in addition to putting your Name on you paper, please add the Date.

5. a my brother tom is twelve years old.
   b my Brother, Tom; is twelve years old.
   c My brother, Tom, is twelve years old.

6. a Varun and i love halloween.
   b Varun and I love Halloween.
   c Varun and I love halloween.

7. a I saw Richard run like the wind.
   b i saw richard run like the wind.
   c I saw richard run like the wind?

8. a When you have finished, eating, clear your place.
   b When you have finished eating clear your place.
   c When you have finished eating, clear your place.

9. a Shell never get her own room if she cant keep it clean.
   b She'll never get her own Room if she can't keep it clean.
   c She'll never get her own room if she can't keep it clean.

10. a "Don't ask questions". said mother to Madhavi.
    b "Don't ask questions", said mother to Madhavi.
    c 'Don't ask question', said mother to madhavi.

Exercise V

Insert capitalisation and punctuation marks in the passage given below.

sharks known to mariners as sea dogs are a group of fish characterised by a cartilaginous skeleton five to seven gill slits on the sides of the head and pectoral fins which are not fused to the head well known species such as the great white shark tiger shark blue shark and the hammerhead shark are apex predators even though their survival is threatened by human related activities they are organisms at the top of their underwater food chain their predatory skill fascinates and frightens humans a sharks teeth are embedded in its gums rather than its jaw they are constantly replaced throughout the sharks life multiple rows of replacement teeth grow in a groove on the inside of the jaw and steadily move forward in comparison to a conveyor belt some sharks lose 30000 or more teeth in their lifetime

Exercise VI

Insert capitalisation and punctuation marks in the passage given below.

Betty Crocker

a large number of todays children do not know who betty crocker is therere a lot of people who used to rely on her cookbooks says my mother true back in the 1930s betty crocker was a name everyone knew however the name betty crocker actually came from an employees imagination marjorie husted said in 1930 well make her look like the average american homemaker betty crockers 101 delicious bisquick creations was the name of one of her books and a television commercial asked whos the person whose cookies we love soon boxes of bettys cake brownie and biscuit mixes appeared on the shelves of supermarkets in 1946 betty crocker was voted the united states second most popular woman eleanor roosevelt was first few people realised that she didnt really exist she was simply general mills icon as womens fashions changed the company updated her picture her appearance became more professional looking as women entered the business world people agreed with the commercial that told them buy betty crocker it's a quality you can trust in honour of this fictitious woman a street was named after her the streets name is betty crocker drive.

3 Prepositions

A preposition is a word which is used before a noun, a noun phrase or a pronoun, connecting it to another word.

We can classify prepositions into these groups

* Prepositions of time, e.g. *in* the 20th century, *at* night, *on* Monday.
* Prepositions of place, e.g. The plates are *on* the table, Rajendra is *in* the garden.
* Prepositions used after some adjectives, verbs or nouns, e.g. Scotland is famous *for* whisky, Sharmila is waiting *for* her friend, Ravi has trouble *with* remembering new words, Kamla went *to* Kashmir *for* her holiday.
* Prepositions used in certain phrases, e.g. Arvind arrived *at* the auditorium just *in* time *for* the programme.
* Complex prepositions, those consisting of more than one word, e.g. Nobody objected *apart from* you, so we went ahead with the agreement.

Practice Centre

Exercise I

Fill in the blanks by choosing the correct prepositions of time from the given options.

1. Lata had promised to be back _________ five o'clock.

   a in   b by
   c past   d ago

2. It's only two weeks _________ Diwali.

   a ago   b for
   c from   d to

3. Many shops don't open _________ Sunday.

   a before   b at
   c on   d to

4. _________ the evenings, I like to relax.

   a In   b Since
   c For   d By

5. The dinosaurs became extinct 70 million years _________ .

   a in   b before
   c since   d ago

6. I'm just going to sleep _________ two hours.

   a for   b from   c till   d by

7. England have not won the World Cup in football _________ 1966.

   a in   b by   c at   d since

8. There is a meeting of all the office staff _________ 2.30 sharp this afternoon.

   a in   b for
   c at   d before

9. My grandmother is always up _________ dawn.

   a for   b from
   c till   d before

10. The Head Office of the company is open _________ 9.30 AM to 6.00 PM, Monday to Friday.

    a from   b for
    c at   d to

Exercise II

Fill in the blanks by choosing the correct prepositions of place from the given options.

1. Kavita held the umbrella ________ both of us to prevent us from getting drenched by the rain.
   - a by
   - b on
   - c over
   - d under

2. The plane is visible just ________ the clouds.
   - a towards
   - b below
   - c onto
   - d from

3. What time does the train _____ Katra arrive at New Delhi station?
   - a above
   - b into
   - c onto
   - d from

4. The explorer Columbus sailed ________ the Atlantic Ocean.
   - a from
   - b between
   - c onto
   - d across

5. The girl who is standing ________ the house is known to me.
   - a under
   - b between
   - c through
   - d beside

6. There is a path ________ the Dal lake leading towards the Shankaracharya temple.
   - a across
   - b above
   - c between
   - d through

7. Lalit ran swiftly ________ the jungle, as he was afraid of wild animals.
   - a under
   - b between
   - c through
   - d on

8. I slipped ________ a banana skin as I stepped onto the road.
   - a from
   - b in
   - c on
   - d into

9. Shall we go ________ the garden to talk it out?
   - a from
   - b on
   - c under
   - d into

10. The cat is sleeping ________ the chair.
    - a from
    - b under
    - c to
    - d between

Exercise III

Fill in the blanks by choosing the correct prepositions used after some adjectives, verbs or nouns from the given options.

1. Are you pleased ________ your new Geography teacher?
   - a from
   - b with
   - c to
   - d about

2. It's great that you got that job - you should be proud ______ yourself.
   - a of
   - b with
   - c in
   - d as

3. Lalita is very pleased ________ her exam results.
   - a from
   - b in
   - c to
   - d with

4. He isn't really interested ________ getting married.
   - a to
   - b on
   - c in
   - d with

5. I'm very proud of my daughter, ________ she worked very hard.
   - a from
   - b as
   - c to
   - d at

6. When we arrived ________ the cinema hall, the film had already started.
   - a from
   - b at
   - c to
   - d on

7. The car belongs ________ my father, so I don't think we can use it.
   - a in
   - b on
   - c to
   - d of

8. Don't worry - I'll pay ________ the tickets.
   - a from
   - b for
   - c to
   - d about

9. Don't worry ________ Ganesh, he'll be fine.
   - a from
   - b at
   - c to
   - d about

10. It's so noisy that I can't concentrate ________ my homework.
    - a on
    - b in
    - c to
    - d about

Exercise IV

Fill in the blanks by choosing the correct prepositions used in certain phrases from the given options.

1. Make no mistake _______ this man, he is a wonderful person.

     a on   b at
     c about   d for

2. All the ladies were making a beeline _______ the bargain sale of sarees.

     a of   b for
     c about   d at

3. You can make a name _______ yourself if you top in the Board exam.

     a of   b for
     c upon   d off

4. Why don't you make a clean breast _______ the fraud you committed?

     a for   b from
     c of   d about

5. Did you make a fool _______ Sandeep to get your revenge?

     a of   b for
     c off   d from

6. Please dress neatly to make an impression _______ your school Principal.

     a at   b on   c upon   d of

7. You have made a hit _______ your friends by showing them your new laptop.

     a upon   b with
     c on   d at

8. You can make inroads _______ the opposite half by passing the ball skilfully.

     a about   b on
     c into   d at

9. Sameer made amends _______ his rude behaviour by apologising in front of everyone.

     a with   b for
     c of   d to

10. You can't make head or tail _______ calculus in class 8.

     a of   b from
     c about   d at

Exercise V

Fill in the blanks by choosing complex prepositions from the given options.

1. Your car was very _______ my car, which caused the accident.

     a ahead of   b close to
     c opposite to

2. You should telephone _______ send an e-mail, just to be sure.

     a as well as   b in addition to
     c moreover

3. We went swimming _______ the cold weather.

     a even though   b in spite of
     c up against

4. Would you like tea _______ coffee?

     a despite of   b instead of
     c in exchange

5. The school is _______ the bank. It is just around the corner.

     a near to
     b next to
     c in front of

6. Everyone came for the party _______ Lalit, who had to stay behind.

     a in addition to   b aside from
     c except for

7. There was a shop here _______ 2005. But it closed that year.

     a up until   b up to
     c prior to

8. Sorry, we're out of lime juice. But we have every fruit juice _______ lime.

     a other than   b in place of
     c out of

9. I'm phoning you _______ Mr Bhatia, I represent him in legal matters.

     a on behalf of   b on account of
     c in place of

10. Nobody is _______ your idea, as it won't work.

     a in favour of   b in addition to
     c along with

Exercise VI

Complete the story by choosing suitable prepositions from those given in the box below. Options for each blank are identified by the numbers allotted to the prepositions in the box. Options are given below the story.

(i) to   (ii) in   (iii) of   (iv) off   (v) about   (vi) with   (vii) for   (viii) on   (ix) at   (x) before

After her husband's demise, an old woman went **1.** _____ live **2.** _____ her son and daughter-in-law and a five years old grandson. The family ate together. But the shaking hands and failing sight **3.** _____ the elderly lady made eating difficult. Grains **4.** _____ rice rolled **5.** _____ her spoon **6.** _____ the floor. When she held the cup **7.** _____ her hand, tea spilled **8.** _____ the floor. The son and daughter-in-law became angry. "Something must be done **9.** _____ mother," said the son. So the husband and wife set a separate place **10.** _____ her **11.** _____ the corner. There, grandmother used **12.** _____ eat her meals alone. Because she happened **13.** _____ break a plate or two, her food was served **14.** _____ a plastic plate. She had tears **15.** _____ her eyes as she sat alone seeing the family glancing **16.** _____ her occasionally. The five years old watched it all **17.** _____ silence. One evening **18.** _____ dinner the couple noticed their son working **19.** _____ wooden scraps **20.** _____ his room. The father asked the child, "What are you making?" Innocently the boy responded: "Oh I am making little bowls **21.** _____ you and mummy **22.** _____ eat your food **23.** _____ once you grow old."

The parents were speechless. They did not utter a word. But that evening, the husband took his mother's hand and gently led her back **24.** _____ the dining table. The grandmother had a radiant smile **25.** _____ her face.

1.	a (i)	b (ii)	**14.**	a (ii)	b (viii)

<table>
<tr><td>1.</td><td>a (i)</td><td>b (ii)</td><td>14.</td><td>a (ii)</td><td>b (viii)</td></tr>
<tr><td></td><td>c (ix)</td><td>d (vi)</td><td></td><td>c (iii)</td><td>d (vi)</td></tr>
<tr><td>2.</td><td>a (vii)</td><td>b (iii)</td><td>15.</td><td>a (i)</td><td>b (iii)</td></tr>
<tr><td></td><td>c (vi)</td><td>d (v)</td><td></td><td>c (vii)</td><td>d (ii)</td></tr>
<tr><td>3.</td><td>a (vii)</td><td>b (viii)</td><td>16.</td><td>a (ii)</td><td>b (ix)</td></tr>
<tr><td></td><td>c (iv)</td><td>d (iii)</td><td></td><td>c (i)</td><td>d (v)</td></tr>
<tr><td>4.</td><td>a (i)</td><td>b (iii)</td><td>17.</td><td>a (vi)</td><td>b (iv)</td></tr>
<tr><td></td><td>c (iv)</td><td>d (v)</td><td></td><td>c (ii)</td><td>d (vii)</td></tr>
<tr><td>5.</td><td>a (iv)</td><td>b (iii)</td><td>18.</td><td>a (iv)</td><td>b (ix)</td></tr>
<tr><td></td><td>c (v)</td><td>d (x)</td><td></td><td>c (v)</td><td>d (x)</td></tr>
<tr><td>6.</td><td>a (iii)</td><td>b (vii)</td><td>19.</td><td>a (vi)</td><td>b (vii)</td></tr>
<tr><td></td><td>c (viii)</td><td>d (ix)</td><td></td><td>c (i)</td><td>d (v)</td></tr>
<tr><td>7.</td><td>a (vii)</td><td>b (ii)</td><td>20.</td><td>a (viii)</td><td>b (ii)</td></tr>
<tr><td></td><td>c (ix)</td><td>d (i)</td><td></td><td>c (vii)</td><td>d (v)</td></tr>
<tr><td>8.</td><td>a (viii)</td><td>b (ix)</td><td>21.</td><td>a (vii)</td><td>b (i)</td></tr>
<tr><td></td><td>c (ii)</td><td>d (iv)</td><td></td><td>c (ii)</td><td>d (vi)</td></tr>
<tr><td>9.</td><td>a (vii)</td><td>b (i)</td><td>22.</td><td>a (ii)</td><td>b (iv)</td></tr>
<tr><td></td><td>c (v)</td><td>d (vi)</td><td></td><td>c (i)</td><td>d (vii)</td></tr>
<tr><td>10.</td><td>a (x)</td><td>b (i)</td><td>23.</td><td>a (ix)</td><td>b (ii)</td></tr>
<tr><td></td><td>c (ii)</td><td>d (vii)</td><td></td><td>c (vii)</td><td>d (vi)</td></tr>
<tr><td>11.</td><td>a (ix)</td><td>b (i)</td><td>24.</td><td>a (vii)</td><td>b (viii)</td></tr>
<tr><td></td><td>c (ii)</td><td>d (viii)</td><td></td><td>c (i)</td><td>d (v)</td></tr>
<tr><td>12.</td><td>a (ii)</td><td>b (iii)</td><td>25.</td><td>a (ii)</td><td>b (iii)</td></tr>
<tr><td></td><td>c (iv)</td><td>d (i)</td><td></td><td>c (iv)</td><td>d (viii)</td></tr>
<tr><td>13.</td><td>a (iii)</td><td>b (i)</td><td></td><td></td><td></td></tr>
<tr><td></td><td>c (ix)</td><td>d (vi)</td><td></td><td></td><td></td></tr>
</table>

④ Determiners

Determiners are used to modify nouns. A determiner indicates reference to something specific or something of a particular type. This function is usually performed by **articles**, **demonstratives**, **possessive determiners** and **quantifiers**.

Determiners are always followed by nouns. Thus, subject pronouns (*I, you, he*, etc) and possessive pronouns (*mine, yours, his*, etc) cannot be determiners because they can never be followed by a noun.

Examples of determiners (*indicated in bold*) are

- **The** woman
- **This** car
- **Some** people

Types of Determiner	Example Words	Example Sentences
Articles	a, an, the	• I have a friend in Mumbai. • I saw an eagle flying. • Close the door, please.
Demonstratives	this, that, these, those	• Those boys are my friends. • That room is dirty.
Possessive *(i) Adjectives* *(ii) Pronouns*	my, your, his, her, its, our, your, their mine, his, hers, yours, ours, theirs	• This is your house. • This car is mine.
Quantifiers	some, any, few, little, more, much, many, each, every, both, all, enough, half, little, whole, less, etc	• Manohar knows more people than Lalit. • Little knowledge is a dangerous thing.

Practice Centre

Exercise I

Replace the personal pronouns (in brackets) with possessive adjectives from the given options.

1. Puneeta likes (she) ______ dog.
   a her b its c my d his

2. She goes to college with (she) ______ brother.
   a their b our c her d his

3. (It) ______ name is Tommy.
   a Your b Our c Her d Its

4. (He) ______ favourite hobby is collecting matchbox labels.
   a His b Her c Our d Its

5. (I) ______ husband and I want to go to Mumbai.
   a Your b My c His d Her

6. Where is (I) ______ school bag?
   a their b its c my d our

7. We want to see (it) ______ historical monuments.
   a their b its c her d our

8. (You) ______ laptop is very expensive.
   a My b Your c His d Her

9. Here is (we) ______ professor.
   a our b their c your d his

10. (They) ______ father works in the government.
    a Its b Their c Her d His

Exercise II

Fill in the blanks with (a) 'some' or (b) 'any'.

1. Would you like _______ more chicken?
2. Go into _______ shop in the market and ask.
3. Did you buy _______ juice?
4. In Kanpur in the winter there's hardly _______ sunlight.
5. Can I have _______ more juice?
6. Could you give me _______ writing paper?
7. I didn't find _______ problem.
8. Do you have _______ sugar?
9. Did you buy _______ vegetables?
10. _______ student will tell you that they don't have enough money.

Exercise III

Fill in the blanks with the proper determiners in the story given below by selecting them from the options given below the story.

Kunti Meets Karna

"War is near.", Krishna told Kunti, "**1.**_____ sons will fight against **2.**_____ cousins. There will be much bloodshed."

Kunti was deeply disturbed. The Pandavas would fight against **3.**_____ Kaurvas and Karna was on Duryodhana's side! Karna would fight against **4.**_____ brothers, perhaps kill them, or be killed himself. He was **5.**_____ precious first born whom she had never acknowledged, never fondled with **6.**_____ mother's love. Despair came into **7.**_____ eyes. Kunti made up **8.**_____ mind to tell Karna **9.**_____ truth. **10.**_____ was **11.**_____ only way to persuade him to leave Duryodhana to fight on **12.**_____ side of **13.**_____ Pandavas. With Karna gone, Duryodhana would be weakened in forces and in spirit. **14.**_____ Pandavas would be able to vanquish him with ease. This was **15.**_____ right time for Karna to learn **16.**_____ secret of **17.**_____ birth.

Kunti hurried to **18.**_____ banks of **19.**_____ Ganga river, where she knew Karna would be at **20.**_____ morning prayers. Karna was at **21.**_____ river bank as Kunti had expected. He was facing east, where **22.**_____ sun had just risen, with **23.**_____ eyes closed. Kunti waited. On **24.**_____ completion of **25.**_____ prayer, Karna opened his eyes. He was surprised to see Kunti.

1.	a	our	b	your	c	hers	**14.**	a	a	b	the	c	their
2.	a	their	b	its	c	yours	**15.**	a	about	b	this	c	the
3.	a	their	b	the	c	his	**16.**	a	the	b	our	c	his
4.	a	her	b	his	c	ours	**17.**	a	his	b	that	c	the
5.	a	a	b	the	c	her	**18.**	a	a	b	an	c	the
6.	a	an	b	a	c	the	**19.**	a	her	b	the	c	its
7.	a	his	b	her	c	their	**20.**	a	his	b	a	c	the
8.	a	its	b	her	c	his	**21.**	a	a	b	the	c	this
9.	a	a	b	the	c	this	**22.**	a	their	b	the	c	his
10.	a	that	b	it	c	this	**23.**	a	its	b	the	c	his
11.	a	this	b	that	c	the	**24.**	a	his	b	her	c	the
12.	a	his	b	our	c	the	**25.**	a	its	b	his	c	hers
13.	a	our	b	this	c	the							

Exercise IV

Choose between 'a', 'an', 'the' and 'no article' to fill in the blanks.

- Mark option (a) as answer if you choose 'a' to fill the gap.
- Mark option (b) as answer if you choose 'an' to fill the gap.
- Mark option (c) as answers if you choose 'the' to fill the gap.
- Mark option (d) as answer if you choose 'no article' to fill the gap.

1. When Sarvesh was a child, he went to school in _____ Delhi.

2. Brajendra can't afford to go to a foreign country on holiday this year. So he's going to have ____ UP holiday this year.

3. Could you pass me ____ sugar, please?

4. I don't know why they are building ____ hospital in the city centre. It already has three hospitals.

5. Shashi, Parveen is on ____ phone. She wants to ask you a question.

6. Karan was ____ heir to a large fortune.

7. When Ashok got home from school, he went into his room, put his bag on ____ floor and sat in his favourite rocking chair.

8. I need _____ new shoes. These ones are old and they have holes in them.

9. Govind wanted to visit _____ European city. So he decided to go to Paris.

10. Every week our English speaking teacher gives us _____ MP3 CD with all our listening for the week on it.

Exercise V

Directions Q No. 1-17. *Choose between (a) 'that', (b) 'those', (c) 'this' or (d) 'these' to fill in the blanks in the story. In some blanks there may be more than one option to fill a blank.*

1. _______ incident always reminds me of my poor Uncle Podger. You never saw such a commotion up and down 2. _______ old house of ours in all your life, as when 3. _______ uncle of mine undertook to do a job. 4. _______ picture would have come home from the frame-makers, and be standing in the dining-room, waiting to be put up; and my aunt would ask what was to be done with it, and Uncle Podger would say, "Oh, you leave 5. _______ to me. Don't any of you, worry yourselves about 6. _______. Those worthless nephews will never put it up. I'll do all 7. _______.

And then he would take off 8. _______ dirty coat of his, and begin.

Now you go and get me 9. _______ hammer of mine, Will, he would shout; and you bring me 10. _______ ruler lying over there, Tom; and I shall want 11. _______ step-ladder lying in the basement. I want 12. _______ chair lying in the kitchen, too; and, Jim! You run round to 13. _______ lazy Mr Goggles, and tell him, will he lend him 14. _______ spirit-level of his? And don't you go, Maria, because 15. _______ children of ours have all gone out and I shall want somebody to hand me up the picture, 16. _______ nails and 17. _______ hammer.

5 Verb Tenses

Overview of Verb Tenses with Examples

Simple Present	Simple Past	Simple Future
Mohit plays football every day.	Two years ago, Mohit played football in Mumbai.	(i) If Mohit wants to play football with me, I will play. (ii) I am going to play football next year.
Present Progressive	**Past Progressive**	**Future Progressive**
Shyam is playing football now.	Shyam was playing football when I called yesterday.	(i) Shyam will be playing football tomorrow. (ii) Shyam is going to be playing football tomorrow.
Present Perfect	**Past Perfect**	**Future Perfect**
Karan has played football in many cities.	Karan had played football a little before he moved to Delhi.	Karan will have played football for three hours if he plays for another hour.
Present Perfect Progressive	**Past Perfect Progressive**	**Future Perfect Progressive**
Salim has been playing football for ten years.	Salim had been playing football for three years before he moved to Mumbai.	Salim will have been playing football for over three hours by the time you arrive.

Practice Centre

Exercise I

Fill in the blanks in the telephonic conversation with the correct form of the verb given in brackets just before each blank in present tense.

Bhawna	Hello.
Jagdish	May I please speak to Bhawna?
Bhawna	Yes, this is Bhawna.
Jagdish	Bhawna! How (be) __________ **1.** you? This is Jagdish.
Bhawna	Ahhh …… Jagdish! I (be) __________ **2.** fine. How are you?

Jagdish I'm great, thanks.

Bhawna That (be) __________ **3.** good. So, what's up?

Jagdish Well, I (have) __________ **4.** a problem for you to solve.

Bhawna Sure.

Jagdish My motorcycle (be) __________ **5.** defective. I (try) ________ ________ ________ **6.** to repair it for days. I (no, know) ________ ________ ________ **7.** what is wrong with it. I (no, can, fix) ________ ________ **8.** it.

Bhawna Have you tried to start it?

Jagdish Yes, I (try) ________ ________ **9.** to start it many times, but it just won't start. The motorcycle is pretty new. I just got it last November.

Bhawna   Hmm. Well, what (happen) _________ **10.** when you try to start it? What kind of noise does it make?

Jagdish   It (make) _________ **11.** a strange sound. Then the engine (die) _________ **12.**.

Bhawna   Okay. (You, stand) _________ _________ _________ **13.** beside it right now?

Jagdish   Yes.

Bhawna   Okay. There are some things that you need to check. First, you need to inspect the spark plugs.

Jagdish   Hold on. Okay, I (inspect) _________ _________ **14.** them under a light now. They look clean.

Bhawna   Okay, that's good. Now you need to test the battery. (You, have) _________ _________ _________ **15.** a battery tester?

Jagdish   Yes, I do. My brother got me one for my birthday. Let's see…okay, I (use) _________ _________ **16.** it right now. The battery (appear) _________ **17.** to be full of life.

Bhawna   Hmm. That is strange. I (wonder) _________ **18.** what the problem could be!

Jagdish   Yes…very strange.

Bhawna   That's too bad. Well, there (be) _________ **19.** one more thing you can check.

Jagdish   Well, what is it?

Bhawna   The petrol level.

Jagdish   Wait! I (not, check) _________ _________ _________ **20.** that yet! Hold on! I (check) _________ _________ **21.** the petrol level now.

Bhawna   Well, what (do) _________ **22.** it look like?

Jagdish   It (look) _________ **23.** empty! Wow, that (be) _________ **24.** the problem. How embarrassing. I am sorry that I bothered you about this!

Bhawna   That's okay. The same thing (happen) _________ _________ **25.** to me with my scooter. You had better go get some petrol! Talk to you later! Bye!

Jagdish   Okay, thanks! Bye!

1.	a	is	b	are	c	do	d	goes
2.	a	is	b	am	c	are	d	was
3.	a	is	b	am	c	were	d	are
4.	a	have	b	has	c	had	d	am having
5.	a	has	b	is	c	are	d	was
6.	a	has been trying	b	has tried	c	have been trying	d	am trying
7.	a	did not know	b	do not know	c	known	d	knowing
8.	a	cannot fix	b	couldn't fix	c	get it fixed	d	fix
9.	a	has tried	b	have tried	c	had tried	d	have been trying
10.	a	happens	b	happened	c	is happening	d	will be happening
11.	a	is making	b	made	c	makes	d	will be making
12.	a	dies	b	died	c	will have died	d	is dying
13.	a	Are you standing	b	Is you standing	c	You are standing	d	You been standing
14.	a	is inspecting	b	am inspecting	c	will be inspecting	d	are inspecting
15.	a	Did you have	b	Do you have	c	Are you having	d	Do yourself have
16.	a	is using	b	am using	c	are using	d	will be using
17.	a	appears	b	appeared	c	is appearing	d	appeared
18.	a	wondering	b	wonder	c	am wondering	d	is wondering
19.	a	is	b	am	c	are	d	was
20.	a	have not checked	b	has not checked	c	had not checked	d	have been checked
21.	a	haven't checked	b	am checking	c	is checking	d	checked

22.	a	do	b	did	c	does	d	is
23.	a	looks	b	looking	c	have looked	d	look
24.	a	has been	b	is	c	are	d	was
25.	a	has happened	b	happens	c	had happened	d	happening

Exercise II

Fill in the spaces with the correct form of the verb in any aspect of the past tense.

Mustaq and Shabnam are brother and sister. They (grow) __________ **1.** up together in the city that used to be known as Calcutta, in West Bengal. Mustaq (move) __________ **2.** to Pakistan after partition in 1947.

Shabnam and her family (visit) __________ **3.** Mustaq and his family last year. Shabnam's family (fly) __________ **4.** from Kolkata to Lahore for the visit. Although the children (never, meet) _______ _______ _________ **5.** before, writing to each other only through e-mail, the families (have) _________ **6.** a great time together.

Every day for a week, the adults and the children (play) _______ _________ **7.**, talking, and eating together. One day, they (cook) _________ **8.** some Indian recipes that (be) _______ _________ **9.** in the family for generations. For years, Shabnam (save) _______ _________ _________ **10.** them and treasuring them in a box their mother (give) _______ _________ **11.** her just before she (die) _______ **12..** One of their mother's favourites (be) _______ _________ **13.** a dessert called mango custard.

One night after everyone else (already, go) _______ _______ _________ **14.** to bed, Mustaq and Shabnam (quietly, sit) _______ _______ _________ **15.** and talking.

"What have you (miss) _________ **16.** most about Kolkata?" Shabnam wanted to know.

Mustaq (pause) _________ **17.**, then answered, "Mostly, I miss living in a city with such wonderful landmarks. The kids and I (look) _______ _______ _________ **18.** at some books about Kolkata and India for a while before you and your family (arrive) _________ **19..**

1.	a	had grown	b	grew	c	were grown	d	grown
2.	a	has moved	b	had moved	c	have moved	d	moved
3.	a	visited	b	had visited	c	have visited	d	had been visiting
4.	a	had flown	b	have flown	c	flew	d	has flown
5.	a	met	b	did not meet	c	had never met	d	have never met
6.	a	had	b	has	c	have been	d	have
7.	a	were playing	b	playing	c	is playing	d	am playing
8.	a	has cooked	b	cooked	c	have cooked	d	had cooked
9.	a	had been	b	has been	c	have been	d	would have been
10.	a	had been saving	b	has saved	c	had saved	d	has been saving
11.	a	gave	b	given	c	had given	d	had been giving
12.	a	died	b	had died	c	have died	d	has been dead
13.	a	had been	b	has been	c	have been	d	were
14.	a	had already gone	b	has gone	c	gone	d	have gone
15.	a	are quietly sitting	b	were quietly sitting	c	was sitting	d	had been sitting
16.	a	had missed	b	have missed	c	missed	d	missing
17.	a	paused	b	had paused	c	have paused	d	was paused
18.	a	had been looking	b	have been looking	c	has been looking	d	were looking
19.	a	had arrived	b	arrived	c	have arrived	d	arriving

ENGLISH **OLYMPIAD** CLASS VIII

Exercise III

Fill in the spaces with the correct form of the verb in any aspect of the future tense.

Sunita has been training her dog, Tommy, for competition for the past six months. Sunita is Tommy's "handler," and together they are a team. If Tommy is ready, Sunita (take) _________ _________**1.** him to a dog show in Mumbai in September.

Sunita imagines the upcoming dog show. She has many questions about it. She decides to ask one of her friends, Sarla, about it.

"What _________**2.** I (do) _________ _________**3.** at the show, exactly?" she asks.

"You (compete) _________ _________ _________**4.** against other teams as they complete a course of challenging exercises," Sarla tells her. "The exercises at the show (involve) _________ _________ _________ _________**5.** giving commands, jumping, pivoting, spiraling, side stepping, and dropping. Each exercise (be) _________ _________ _________ _________**6.** numbered. As they are doing the exercises together, the handlers (talk) _________ _________ _________**7.** to their dogs."

"Before beginning the course," Sarla continues, "Each team (receive) _________ _________**8.** 200 points. Each time a team makes a mistake, a point is deducted by the judge. At the end of the course, the handlers (probably, praise) _________ _________ _________**9.** their dogs and give them food as rewards. The teams (do) _________ _________ _________**10.** their best together, and therefore will deserve a rest. By the time the dogs finish eating, the judge (tally) _________ _________ _________**11.** each team's final score."

"The dogs at the show will not only be of good breeds. Lots of mixed-breed dogs (surely, participate) _________ _________ _________ _________**12.** in the show, too. There is no age limit for the dogs, either, and it has been decided that all future shows (include) _________ _________ _________ _________**13.** a division for handlers of ages 8 to 18. This way, children can get more involved."

Sunita is 19 years old, and Tommy is 10. He is a Labrador mix. If they go to the show, they (enter) _________ _________**14.** the Level 1 competition, because it (be) _________ _________**15.** their first competition. This dog show also includes Levels 2 and 3. 3 is the highest level.

Sunita has a plan. She says that she (decide) _________ _________ _________ _________**16.** by July whether Tommy is ready to compete. By then, she (train) _________ _________ _________ _________**17.** him for eight months. She hopes they (win) _________ _________**18.** a blue ribbon!

1.	a	shall take	b	will take	c	taking	d are taking
2.	a	will	b	am	c	have	d is
3.	a	am doing	b	is doing	c	be doing	d doing
4.	a	shall be competing	b	will be competing	c	competing	d are competing
5.	a	involve	b	will involve	c	will be involving	d are going to involve
6.	a	is going to be	b	will be	c	are going	d is going to be
7.	a	shall be talking	b	talking	c	will be talking	d are talking
8.	a	will receive	b	will have received	c	receive	d receiving
9.	a	will probably praise	b	shall probably praise	c	are probably praising	d will be probably praising
10.	a	would have done	b	will have done	c	will be doing	d doing
11.	a	will be tallying	b	will have tallied	c	shall have tallied	d would be tallying
12.	a	will surely be participating			b	will surely have participated	
	c	would have participated			d	participating	
13.	a	are going to include	b	will include	c	will have included	d would have included

14.	a shall enter	b will enter	c will have entered	d would have entered
15.	a is	b has been	c will be	d had been
16.	a will be deciding	b is going to decide	c will have decided	d deciding
17.	a would have trained	b will have trained	c will be trained	d trained
18.	a will win	b shall win	c will have won	d would have won

Exercise IV

Fill in the spaces with the correct form of the verb by selecting the correct option.

1. Who ________ food in your family when your mother is not at home?
   a cooks
   b is cooking
   c has been cooking
   d cooked

2. Where is John? He ______ his car in the garage.
   a repairs
   b is repairing
   c has repaired
   d repaired

3. She ________ the living room when she heard a strange noise in the kitchen.
   a has cleaned
   b has been cleaning
   c was cleaning
   d had cleaned

4. I envy you. At five tomorrow you ________ some suntan on a nice beach in Goa.
   a will get
   b will be getting
   c will have gotten
   d will have been getting

5. You arrived two days ago. You are going to leave next Sunday. By the time you leave, you ________ nine days here.
   a spend
   b have spent
   c are spending
   d will have spent

6. Where is he? I ________ for him since three o'clock!
   a am waiting
   b have been waiting
   c was waiting
   d had been waiting

7. I went to Singapore last month. I ________ there before. It's a beautiful country.
   a have never been
   b had never been
   c never was
   d never been

8. He said that his mother would be very upset when she ________ that he had lost his job.
   a learns
   b learned
   c had learned
   d would learn

9. She said she ________ late at the office that evening and that she ________ home till about eleven.
   a is working / got
   b was working / gets
   c would be working / wouldn't get
   d will be working / was getting

10. As soon as there ________ even a temporary break in the weather the climbers ________ their attempt to reach the summit.
   a is / will renew
   b was / renew
   c will be / renewed
   d is / renewed

11. In the evenings, I often play chess with my next door neighbour. I ________ chess with him ever since I ________ to live here ten years ago.
   a have been playing / came
   b play / came
   c am playing / have come
   d have played / have come

12. Anuradha ________ her driving test three times because she's so bad at reversing. But she ________ reversing since last week and I think she has got better at it.
   a has failed / has been practising
   b failed / practised
   c failed / was practising
   d fails / practises

13. I have been waiting for the prices of the houses to come down before buying one, but I think I ________ too long and the prices ________ to go up again.
   a wait / began
   b am waiting / began
   c have waited / are beginning
   d waited / were beginning

ENGLISH **OLYMPIAD** CLASS VIII

14. Recently I experienced how tedious long
    plane trips could be. I ________ in an airplane
    for fairly long distances before, but never as
    long as when I went to America last month.
    - a have never flown
    - b didn't fly
    - c have flown
    - d hadn't flown

15. This bicycle ________ in our family for
    fourteen years. My father used it for the first
    five years, my brother rode it for the next
    five and I ________ it for the last four.
    - a is / have had
    - b had been / had
    - c was / had had
    - d has been / had

16. It's a great pity you didn't come to London
    with us last summer. As you ______ it before,
    it ________ a wonderful holiday for you.
    - a hadn't seen / would have been
    - b have never seen / will surely be
    - c didn't see / has been
    - d haven't seen / was

17. Yesterday at a restaurant, I saw Sameera, an
    old friend of mine. I had not seen her for
    years. At first, I ________ her because she
    ________ at least 20 kilos.
    - a didn't recognise / lost
    - b didn't recognise / had lost
    - c hadn't recognised / lost
    - d haven't recognised / had lost

18. Our sailing club is trying to raise money to
    buy a new lifeboat. By the end of the year,
    we ________ out 500 letters asking for
    contributions.
    - a were to send
    - b will send
    - c will be sending
    - d will have been sending

19. Early signs of the rebirth of civilisation in
    Western Europe ________ to appear in the
    11th century as trade ________ again in Italy.
    - a were beginning / will start
    - b began / started
    - c would begin / starts
    - d begin / was starting

20. When a group ________ to a new country, its
    members ________ that they have to modify
    their way of life, including their celebrations
    of significant events.
    - a will immigrate / find
    - b are immigrating / will be found
    - c immigrate / find
    - d were immigrating / found

21. When he ________ that his nomination would
    mean competing with his closest friend he
    ________ to withdraw.
    - a realises / will be decided
    - b realised / was deciding
    - c will realise / decides
    - d realised / decided

22. Computers that once ________ up entire
    rooms ________ now small enough to put on
    desktops and into wristwatches.
    - a took / are
    - b were taking / would be
    - c will take / will be
    - d are taking / will be

23. The immune system ________ by
    distinguishing between the body's own
    materials and things that ________ foreign to
    the body.
    - a works / would be
    - b will be working / are
    - c works / are
    - d was working / will be

24. Despite the multi-religious nature of the
    nation, it ________ that most inhabitants of
    the country ________ common ancestors.
    - a will seem / will share
    - b seems / share
    - c seemed / will share
    - d seems / were sharing

25. The minute we ________ his gift we ________
    him a note of thanks.
    - a received / wrote
    - b are receiving / wrote
    - c will receive / would write
    - d were receiving / wrote

Word Meaning in Context

Some words which we come across every day during our reading of newspapers, magazines, books, etc are simple, normally used words. However, there are many words, e.g. *ambivalent, incessant* or *vitiate*, which are difficult to understand as they are not used often. This in turn reduces our understanding of the sentence as a whole.

In such cases, we will have to make a guess of the meaning of the word, based on what we feel the sentence is wanting to say. In exercises of this type, we will be given four choices for the exact meaning of the word in the context of the sentence.

Two examples are given below to clarify how we should go about answering such questions correctly. Select the best option which is closest in meaning to the underlined word in the sentence given below:

Example 1 I prefer the occasional disturbance of ear-splitting thunder to the <u>incessant</u> dripping of our kitchen sink.

  (a) Harmless   (b) Exciting   (c) Non-stop   (d) Repeated

Answer (c) In the sentence above, the context, i.e., the words surrounding the unfamiliar word provide clues to the word's meaning. The dictionary meaning of incessant is 'never stopping' or 'constant'. Thus, 'non-stop' is the best option.

Example 2 "You told me to use my <u>initiative</u> if I needed money, so I sold our car."

  (a) anger   (b) willpower   (c) proposal   (d) resourcefulness

Answer (d) The dictionary meaning of initiative is 'the ability to decide and act on your own'. Thus, 'resourcefulness' is the best option.

Practice Centre

In each of the following questions, select the best option which is closest in meaning to the underlined word in the sentence.

1. Many of us have <u>ambivalent</u> feelings about our politicians, admiring but also distrusting them.

  a approving   b critical
  c disturbing   d mixed

2. Some animals like the giant land tortoise have remarkable <u>longevity</u>, as they can live several hundred years.

  a length of life   b appearance
  c habits   d body length

3. <u>Mundane</u> activities such as washing clothes or dishes, going shopping for groceries or reading the daily newspaper, all help me relax.

  a exciting   b painful
  c routine   d spiritual

4. Some mentally ill people have <u>bizarre</u> ideas like thinking that the TV is talking to them or that others can steal their thoughts.

  a limited   b strange
  c ordinary   d brilliant

5. Nocturnal creatures such as bats and owls have highly developed senses that enable them to function in the dark.

    a feathery   b brainy
    c active at night   d living

6. Before the advent of television, people spent more time on diversions such as going to watch sports events and movies, visiting relatives and friends, as well as playing board games.

    a occupations   b amusements
    c differences   d duties

7. The Chinese government provides incentives like financial help and free medical care for married couples having only one child.

    a inducements   b deterrents
    c penalties   d warnings

8. Today was a day of turmoil in our office, as the phones were constantly ringing, people were running back and forth, and electrical repairs were being carried out.

    a discussion   b confusion
    c harmony   d peacefulness

9. Changes in such abilities as learning, reasoning, thinking, and language are aspects of cognitive development.

    a physical   b spiritual
    c mental   d materialistic

10. Children who move to a foreign country adapt much more easily than their parents, soon picking up the language and customs of their new home.

    a adjust   b struggle
    c become bored   d retaliate

11. A former employee of the company, irate over having been fired, barged into their factory and damaged some costly machines.

    a undecided   b relieved
    c very angry   d happy

12. The car wash we organised to raise funds for our workshop was a fiasco, as it rained all day.

    a financial success   b welcome surprise
    c mess   d complete disaster

13. "My doctor said that smoking could terminate my life. But I told him, "Everybody's life has to end sometime."

    a extremity   b end
    c climax   d call off

14. As soon as I made a flippant remark to my boss, I regretted sounding so disrespectful.

    a serious   b idiotic
    c disrespectful   d useful

15. Many people have pointed out the harmful effects that a working mother may have on the family, yet there are many salutary effects as well.

    a beneficial   b hurtful
    c well-known   d healthy

16. During their training, police officers must respond to simulated emergencies in preparation for dealing with real ones.

    a mild   b actual
    c bogus   d made up

17. Because trying to control everything our teenagers do can impede their growth, we must allow them to make some decisions on their own to advance their development.

    a predict   b increase
    c barricade   d slow down

18. As remaining stagnant results in loss of strength and health, elderly people need to stay active to remain healthy.

    a unhealthy   b inactive
    c lively   d static

19. Being raised with conflicting values can be a detriment to boys' and girls' relationships with each other, whereas shared values can be beneficial.

    a drawback   b improvement
    c mischief   d relationship

20. While houses and antiques often increase in value, most things, such as cars and mobile phones, depreciate.

    a remain useful
    b break
    c lose value
    d become rubbish

Error Detection

The correct answer to any error detection question will have

1. No grammatical mistakes.
2. Correct sentence structure.
3. No diction errors.
4. No changes to the sentence's intended meaning.

You should employ the process of elimination of unlikely options wherever possible. The easiest way to use thus in sentence correction questions is simply to eliminate any answer choices that are themselves grammatically incorrect. You can also eliminate any choices that alter the intended meaning of the sentence.

Types of Error Detection

Two types of error detection questions are covered below:

Type 1. Identifying the Mistake

Each sentence has been divided into four parts, namely A, B, C and D. One of these parts carries a mistake, which may be a grammatical, punctuation or spelling mistake. Select the part which carries the mistake. In case the sentence is fully correct, write the option as 'E'.

Examples with explanation are given below:

Example 1

As the train was leaving the station, someone pulled the alarm chain and it stopped a few yards
       A   B   C   D
from the platform.

Answer *(D) The phrase should be 'a few yards beyond the platform', as the train was leaving the station.*

Example 2

The High Court awarded the death sentence for all the three accused in the triple murder case.
       A   B   C   D

Answer *(B) The phrase should be 'the death sentence to', as the correct preposition to be used here is 'to', not 'for'.*

Type 2. Select the Incorrect Option

Underlined parts of the given sentences may contain an error in grammar usage, diction or idiom. Select the part that is incorrect by writing the letter (A, B, C or D) by which it is identified.

An example with explanation of the error is given below:

Example

The minutes of the meeting was(A) circulated, but nobody (B) responded; hence (C) no action was (D) taken.

Answer *(A) The word 'minutes' is plural.*

Practice Centre

Exercise I

Each sentence has been divided into four parts, namely A, B, C and D. One of these parts carries a mistake, which may be a grammatical, punctuation or spelling mistake. Select the part which carries the mistake. In case the sentence is fully correct, write the option as 'E'.

1. She was conscious to all that was going on around her house.
   A   B   C   D

2. Sarla is grateful of her uncle for the moral and material support on his part to enable her to continue her
   A   B   C   D
   higher studies.

3. We use to go to the college ground every evening to play football.
   A   B   C   D

4. This pen is better from your pen, as it writes very fluently.
   A   B   C   D

5. We do not want to go for participating into the rally at Jantar Mantar.
   A   B   C   D

6. Bhaskar was suffering with fever for the last few days and had not come to school.
   A   B   C   D

7. There were long queues on the booking windows of cinema halls on the eve of Holi.
   A   B   C   D

8. Mohan was taken with surprise to see Harish wearing a new uniform.
   A   B   C   D

9. The flood has taken a toll of more than a hundred lives in Kashmir and has made much havoc there.
                A   B   C   D

10. If you are not conversant with the work, how can you do even your routine office work in that department?
           A   B   C   D

11. The US sponsored move to boycott the Moscow Olympics failed in spite of the massive propaganda of
                    A   B   C   D
    their part.

12. The Twelfth Five-Year Plan lays stress for employment schemes and provides a rural bias for
                       A   B   C   D
    development.

13. I won't mind if you enter my room without prior permission except when I am busy to study.
           A   B   C   D

14. The prospects of peace between Iraq and the ISIS rebels are not so bright as the danger of further
                  A   B   C   D
    escalation of the war.

15. The number of trains on almost all the important routes have been increased, but every train goes packed.
            A   B   C   D

16. The dictionary, as well as the textbook, were missing from the room.
       A   B   C   D

17. I can't hardly wait for Saturday to come so that we can go to watch the ODI at Brabourne Stadium.
              A   B   C   D

18. The price of onions is going up at the open market because there is not enough stock of the vegetable for
         A   B   C   D

everybody.

19. What do you think for the person I had recommended for a job in your office?
        A   B   C   D

20. Our school requires every student to bring their own instrument box for the geometric drawing classes.
       A   B   C   D

Exercise II

Underlined parts of the given sentences may contain an error in grammar usage, diction or idiom. Select the part that is incorrect by writing the letter (A, B, C or D) by which it is identified.

1. It must(A) be him(B) with whom(C) you enjoy to do(D) your project.

2. Competence(A) without willingness(B) yields(C) in(D) a half-hearted result.

3. The caustic(A) remarks(B) Aditi made was totally(C) uncalled for(D).

4. The reason for(A) my prolonged absence(B) from class was(C) because(D) I was ill for three weeks.

5. Kapil had begun(A) the sea voyage with a mission of(B) exploration, but that(C) quickly became a mission for(D) survival.

6. Tagore's ability to summarise(A) the range of(B) human emotions in simple yet profound(C) eloquent verse is perhaps the greatest reason for his enduring(D) popularity.

7. Determination(A) of the long term effects(B) of CFCs on the upper atmosphere are(C) currently one of the most challenging(D) problems in climate research.

8. The list containing(A) names of miscreants(B) have(C) been submitted to the school Principal for(D) action.

9. Since we were caught completely unawares(A), the affect(B) of the Director's remark was startling(C): some were shocked, but(D) others were angry.

10. We were terrified (A) by sounds: the screaming of (B) the wind, the restless rustle (C) of the leaves in the trees; and the sudden overwhelming (D) explosions of thunder.

11. Although (A) Nepal is rich in scenic beauty (B), it has yet to become a major (C), attraction for global tourists because it did not have (D) adequate facilities to attract them.

12. She managed to enter (A) her house, bolted the door (B) from inside and slump on (D)

8 Connectors

Sentence connectors are used to express relationships between ideas and to combine sentences. In a complex sentence structure, sentence connectors enable us to make more sophisticated sentences.

Example "Mumbai is a very exciting city; **nevertheless,** it is also very expensive" or "**Despite** the fact that Mumbai is very expensive, it is very exciting"

Here, 'nevertheless' and 'Despite' are connectors.

The various types of connectors are

1. **Coordinating Conjunctions** These are used to join two items/clauses of equal importance. *Examples are*

for	and	nor	but	or
yet	so			

2. **Subordinating Conjunctions** They connect a dependent clause and an independent clause by establishing a relationship between them. *Examples are*

after	if	though	although
if only	till	in order that	as
unless	as if	now that	until
as long as	once	as though	when
rather than	whenever	because	since
where	before	so that	whereas
even if	even though	wherever	than
that	while		

3. **Correlative Conjunctions**   They connect equal sentence elements together (like two nouns) and are always composed of two words /phrases. *Examples are*

both…and ……	not…but ……	neither…nor …..	as…as …..
not only…but also ..	either…or …..	whether…or …..	

4. **Linking Adverbs and Transition Words**   They connect two independent clauses or sentences and provide transition between ideas. *Examples are*

accordingly	however	nonetheless	also
indeed	otherwise	beside	instead
similarly	consequently	likewise	still
conversely	meanwhile	subsequently	finally
moreover	then	furthermore	nevertheless
therefore	hence	next	thus

Practice Centre

Exercise I

Fill in the blanks with suitable Coordinating Conjunctions.

1. After a long day at work, Mr Mittal comes home ____ relaxes for a while.
   - a but
   - b and
   - c although
   - d or

2. He is usually very talkative, ____ rather tired.
   - a but
   - b yet
   - c though
   - d and

3. He talks about his activities at the office constantly ____ in detail.
   - a though
   - b although
   - c and
   - d but

4. He never asks about Mrs Mittal's day ____ her problems.
   - a nor
   - b neither
   - c either
   - d not

5. Then he asks her for a cup of tea ____ coffee.
   - a or
   - b and
   - c but
   - d for

6. She tells him he can get it himself ____ do her a favour in the future by always getting it himself.
   - a but
   - b yet
   - c and
   - d either

7. He laughs, ____ she tells him she is serious about what she said.
   - a and
   - b but
   - c though
   - d inspite of

8. He tells her that she's crazy, ____ she tells him that she's leaving.
   - a so
   - b so that
   - c as
   - d and

9. She tells him that, ____ gets him his cup of tea anyway.
   - a and
   - b so
   - c but
   - d because

10. They have been married for six years now, ____ he treats her like a servant.
    - a yet
    - b and
    - c but
    - d though

Exercise II

Fill in the blanks with suitable Subordinating Conjunctions and transition words from the given options.

1. I heard some news on the radio about a fire in our neighbourhood, ____ my family saw it on TV later.
   - a when
   - b as though
   - c though
   - d once

2. They said that it was ____ a laptop computer exploded.
   - a even if
   - b because
   - c before
   - d in order that

3. The fire brigade called in all their men ____ they could douse the flames.
   - a even if
   - b whereas
   - c although
   - d so that

4. The building became engulfed in flames quickly ____ they arrived.
   - a before
   - b after
   - c when
   - d unless

5. However, they sprayed water on the flames ____ they got a chance.
   - a even though
   - b although
   - c whenever
   - d rather than

6. ____ the residents felt the fire was accidental, the police wanted to investigate the cause.
   - a After
   - b Whereas
   - c That
   - d Once

7. ____ they could examine the evidence, they called in their dog squad, which found the source of the fire as a burned-out laptop computer.
   - a Before
   - b If
   - c Unless
   - d In order that

8. ____ the police want to close the case as an accident, the residents are not in agreement.
   - a Now that
   - b If
   - c As though
   - d Although

9. ____ they do not have a roof over their heads, they will not rest till they find the owner of the laptop.
   - a Now that
   - b If
   - c As though
   - d Although

10. ____, they will approach the insurance company which has insured the building against fire for compensation.
    - a Now that
    - b Furthermore
    - c As though
    - d Although

ENGLISH **OLYMPIAD** CLASS VIII

Exercise III

Fill in the blanks with Correlative Conjunctions by selecting the correct option. The number given against each option refers to the corresponding conjunctions given in the box below.

(i) Both, and	(ii) either, or	(iii) not only, but also	(iv) Neither, nor
(v) Whether, or	(vi) as, as	(vii) not, but	(viii) Not only, but also

1. ____ my sister ____ I are brilliant students.
   - a (i)
   - b (ii)
   - c (iii)
   - d (iv)

2. Every term, ____ my sister ____ I win an achievement award.
   - a (vi)
   - b (ii)
   - c (iii)
   - d (v)

3. Last year, my sister ____ won the 'Best in Academics' award, ____ she won the 'Best in Sports' award.
   - a (i)
   - b (ii)
   - c (iii)
   - d (iv)

4. ____ he ____ I want to lose at anything. We're very competitive.
   - a (i)
   - b (ii)
   - c (iii)
   - d (iv)

5. ____ do our parents encourage us to work hard, ____ they reward us when we succeed.
   - a (i)
   - b (ii)
   - c (viii)
   - d (iv)

6. ____ my sister ____ I want to disappoint them.
   - a (i)
   - b (ii)
   - c (iii)
   - d (iv)

7. ____ my father ____ my uncle are lawyers.
   - a (i)
   - b (ii)
   - c (iii)
   - d (iv)

8. ____ I will become a doctor ____ a veterinarian, I'm not sure yet.
   - a (v)
   - b (ii)
   - c (iii)
   - d (iv)

9. I am ____ fond of animals ____ my sister is.
   - a (vi)
   - b (ii)
   - c (iii)
   - d (iv)

10. I'm ____ very athletic in build, ____ my sister is.
    - a (vi)
    - b (vii)
    - c (iii)
    - d (iv)

Exercise IV

Fill in the blanks with suitable Linking Adverbs and Transition Words from the given options.

1. I really don't know why Salil came, __________ I would tell you.
   - a consequently
   - b otherwise
   - c next

2. Jaswant has very little money; __________ his brother Satwant is a millionaire.
   - a hence
   - b conversely
   - c finally

3. Savitri is a very smart woman; __________ it is not at all surprising that she got the job.
   - a consequently
   - b as a result
   - c nonetheless

4. You need to work harder, __________ you'll get fired.
   - a hence
   - b otherwise
   - c moreover

5. He is a very weak President; __________ most people support him.
   - a meanwhile
   - b nevertheless
   - c instead

6. Mohan couldn't tell his wife the truth; __________ he lied.
   - a instead
   - b also
   - c moreover

7. Raveena didn't have all the ingredients to bake a cake; __________ she decided to prepare something else.
   - a accordingly
   - b meanwhile
   - c similarly

8. We wanted to go to the beach; __________ it started to rain and we stayed at home.
   - a however
   - b moreover
   - c similarly

9. We wanted to go to Japan for our holiday; __________ we went to France.
   - a instead
   - b furthermore,
   - c consequently

10. Pratima has a terrible voice; __________ she will go down in history as the worst singer ever.
    - a therefore
    - b nonetheless
    - c still

Exercise V

Fill in the blanks with suitable connectors by selecting the correct option. The number given against each option refers to the corresponding connector given in the box below.

> (i) or   (ii) Before   (iii) and   (iv) nevertheless   (v) then   (vi) when   (vii) but   (viii) even though

1. Don't try to stop us _________ you are going to get hurt!

   a (i)   b (ii)   c (iii)   d (iv)

2. _________ we went to the shopping centre, we went to the park.

   a (i)   b (ii)
   c (iii)   d (iv)

3. _________ you cross the street you must look carefully.

   a (i)   b (ii)
   c (iii)   d (iv)

4. The exam was difficult; _________ Binod passed it easily.

   a (i)   b (ii)
   c (v)   d (iv)

5. First we went to the cinema and _________ we went to a restaurant.

   a (i)   b (vi)   c (v)   d (iv)

6. I didn't know _________ to go.

   a (i)   b (vi)
   c (iii)   d (iv)

7. _________ I have a test I'm always very nervous.

   a (i)   b (ii)
   c (iii)   d (iv)

8. I wanted to visit her _________ I didn't have any time.

   a (v)   b (ii)
   c (iii)   d (vii)

9. We visited Mr Smith _________ he has two ferocious dogs.

   a (viii)   b (ii)
   c (iii)   d (iv)

10. He listened to her carefully _________ then told her what she could do.

    a (viii)   b (vii)   c (iii)   d (iv)

Exercise VI

Fill in the blanks with the suitable connectors in the story given below.

I went to a soccer game today, **1.**_________ it was exciting. I cheered for my team. **2.**_________, they didn't win. My team was playing pretty well, **3.**_________ the other team was too. Both the offense and defence of my team played well **4.**_________ were unlucky. One player fouled another player, **5.**_________ the referee blew his whistle. The striker kicked the ball towards the goal. **6.**_________, it hit the post.

The goalie caught the ball. **7.**_________ he threw it to a teammate. The player hit it with his shoulder, **8.**_________ the referee didn't see it. One player fell down **9.**_________ grabbed his leg **10.**_________ he were hurt. The players hit some great shots; it was exciting.

1.	a but	b and
	c though	d so
2.	a Despite	b In spite
	c But	d Unfortunately
3.	a and	b but
	c because	d as
4.	a nevertheless	b nonetheless
	c moreover	d but
5.	a this	b then
	c and	d so
6.	a While	b Since
	c When	d However
7.	a And	b Then
	c When	d While
8.	a but	b although
	c yet	d because
9.	a despite	b eventhough
	c yet	d and
10.	a as if	b though
	c however	d yet

Logical Sequencing

Logical Sequencing in an Action

Judging the logic of an action means sequencing the given sentences in a logical way, so that the action is logically completed. In such kind of questions, the first and last sentences are identified and the remaining four sentences have to be arranged in order so that the action is logically completed.

Example

In the passage below, the first and last sentences are identified as A and Z. The remaining four sentences are labelled as P, Q, R and S. Find the correct sequence of these four sentences and select the correct option accordingly.

A When pedestrians cross a busy road crossing, they should obey the traffic signals.
P When the pedestrian light turns green, they should walk across when the road is clear.
Q If the road is not clear they should wait.
R They should locate the zebra crossing and look at the signal lights.
S If there are no signal lights, they should look on both sides of the road before walking across.
Z They must not run while crossing the road.

   (a) PQRS   (b) QPSR   (c) RPQS   (d) RSQP

Ans.

c

Out of the four options given, this is the only one possible. The option RSPQ is also possible, but this has not been given as an option.

Practice Centre

In each of the following questions, a passage is given with the first and last sentences identified as A and Z. The remaining four sentences are labelled as P, Q, R and S. Find the correct sequence of these four sentences and select the correct option accordingly.

1. A We see people around us speaking different languages, having different religions and practicing different rituals.
P Besides, look at the myriad forms of dance and music in our country.
Q The intermingling of people has been steadily taking place in India over centuries.
R But within all these diversities, there is an underlying unity, which acts as a cementing force.
S You can also see these diversities in their food habits and dress patterns.
Z A number of people of different racial stock, ethnic backgrounds and religious beliefs have settled down here.

   a PQRS   b PSQR   c SPQR   d SPRQ

2. **A** Gautama Buddha, originally named Siddhartha, was married to Yashodhara at the age of 16.

P He went to the forests and meditated there for 6 years.

Q It was at this place that he attained enlightenment and came to be known as the Buddha.

R But at the age of 29, Gautama Buddha renounced family life to find a solution to the world's continuous sorrow of death, sickness and poverty.

S Thereafter, he went to Bodh Gaya (in Bihar) and meditated under a pipal tree.

Z He then travelled a lot to spread his message and helped people find the path of liberation or freedom.

a PRSQ	b RPSQ
c SRQP	d RSPQ

3. **A** Raga is the basis of classical music.

P Raga is not a true melody scale or any other concept for which an English word exists.

Q It can thus be thought of as an acoustic device to colour the mind of the listener.

R A Raga is based on the principle of a combination of notes selected from the 22 note intervals of the octave.

S It is derived from the Sanskrit word *Ranj*, which means colour.

Z It is a combination of different characteristics which define the Raga.

a PRSQ	b SPQR
c SQRP	d SRQP

4. **A** Have you ever wondered why certain children are bubbling with energy most of the time while others are plain lethargic?

P Moreover, sufficient vitamin D is a strong and powerful guard against pain, inflammation and depression.

Q This energy is reflected in their enthusiasm to do not only their daily activities with aplomb, but also learn and excel at new things.

R In addition to it, it ensures healthy teeth as it helps in the absorption of calcium.

S Such super-active kids score on two counts over their lethargic counterparts - adequate exposure to sunlight and adequate intake of vitamin D, the bone builder vitamin.

Z Furthermore, vitamin D helps regulate blood sugar levels and lowers the blood pressure.

a SQRP	b QPSR
c RPQS	d QSPR

5. **A** A number of great women of India have their names written with golden letters in the history books of India.

P After a son was born to the young princess, tragedy struck the royal household.

Q She was born in a poor family but was married to the son of Malharrao Holkar, the great Maratha Chief, who ruled over Malwa in the middle of the 18th century.

R Rani Ahalyabai is one such lady.

S Both Malharrao and his son were killed in a battle.

Z Thus Ahalyabai was called upon to take up the reins of her state at a very early age.

a RQPS	b QPSR
c RPSQ	d RSQP

6. **A** Some people think parrots can talk because of the structure of their tongue, which is large and thick.

P It may be that this kind of tongue does help them to talk, but it certainly isn't necessary in order for a bird to be able to talk.

Q Hawks and eagles do have such tongues and can't talk!

R Is it because parrots are more intelligent than other birds?

S Other 'talking' birds, such as mynas, crows and ravens, don't have large, thick tongues.

Z This doesn't seem to be the reason either.

a PQRS	b PSQR
c SPRQ	d RPQS

7. **A** A lemming is a very unusual animal found in very cold parts of the world.

P They jump in and start swimming, and they keep swimming, until at last they are so tired that they have to stop swimming.

Q And then, of course, they drown.

R They cross fields and woods, and they swim across streams and rivers, until, after several months of travelling, they reach the sea.

S Once in every few years, the lemmings leave their homes in the mountains and start travelling.

Z Hundreds and thousands of lemmings drown in this fashion.

a SRPQ
b SPRQ
c RPQS
d RSQP

ENGLISH **OLYMPIAD** CLASS VIII

8. A Hibernation is more than sleep.

P The first is that it stores a lot of fat in its body during summer and autumn.

Q It is a very deep sleep.

R The answer lies in two facts.

S Hibernating in this way, the animal can sleep all through the winter without eating for many months.

Z The second is related to the main use the body makes of food - to supply the energy for movement.

    a SQRP   **b** PQRS   **c** PRQS   **d** QSRP

9. A Human speech is a very complicated process, which no animal can perform.

P One reason is that in a very special way, we use a whole series of organs to produce the sounds we want to make when we utter words.

Q They cannot produce a whole series of words to make a sentence.

R And there is another, perhaps more important reason why animals can't talk.

S The way our vocal cords, throat, mouth, nasal cavities, lips, teeth, lower jaw, tongue and palate are moved just to make vowel and consonant sounds, is something animals can't do.

Z Words are only labels for objects, actions, feelings, expressions and ideas.

    a QSPR   **b** PQRS   **c** PSQR   **d** PRSQ

10. A It is now more than 65 years since the British left our country and we became a free nation.

P But sadly, the West still dominates our way of life and thinking.

Q The younger generation apes everything that is typical of Western culture.

R By doing so, they think they can give an impression of being modern.

S The youngsters ape the fashion of the Western people by copying their dresses, music, dances and even their food habits.

Z But to me, the fact is quite the opposite.

    a PSQR   **b** PQSR   **c** PQRS   **d** SRQP

Logical Sequencing in a Process

Judging the logic of the completion of a process means sequencing the given sentences in a logical way, so that the process is logically completed. In such kind of questions, the first and last sentences are identified and the remaining four sentences have to be arranged in order so that the process is logically completed.

Example

The process of baking a cake is given below, the description of the process is divided into six parts with the first and last parts identified as A and Z. The remaining four parts of the process are labelled as P, Q, R and S. Find the correct sequence of these four parts and select the correct option accordingly.

A Collect the ingredients like flour, baking soda, sugar, salt, honey, butter, cardamom , eggs and confectioner's sugar.

P Cool on a wire rack for 10 minutes. Turn out of pan onto a cutting board or baking sheet; invert cake onto rack, top side up.

Q Preheat oven to 200℃. In a large bowl, whisk together flour, baking soda, salt and cardamom and set aside.

R Coat a non-stick pan with cooking oil. Spoon batter into pan; smooth its top. Bake until a toothpick inserted in the middle comes out clean (but slightly wet), may be for 45 minutes.

S In an electric mixer, beat butter, sugar and honey until light and fluffy. Add eggs, one at a time, beating until combined. With mixer on low speed, gradually add flour mixture; beat just until combined.

Z Cool completely. Dust with confectioners' sugar before serving.

    a PSQR   **b** SRQP   **c** SQRP   **d** QSRP

Ans. **d**

Out of the four options given, this is the only one possible.

Practice Centre

In each of the following questions, the description of a process is divided into six parts with the first and last sentences identified as A and Z. The remaining four parts of the process are labelled as P, Q, R and S. Find the correct sequence of these four parts and select the correct option accordingly.

1. Pasting Wallpaper

A Using a plumb line and pencil, draw a line down the wall on which you will be pasting the wallpaper.

P Place the edge of the wallpaper against the line drawn on the wall with the pasted side towards the wall, checking that you are placing its top up against the ceiling.

Q Slide the wallpaper into position so that it goes down absolutely straight.

R Apply paste uniformly to the back of the wallpaper.

S Cut a piece of wallpaper 20 cm longer than what you need.

Z Then smooth down the middle of the wallpaper with a smoothing brush or soft sponge. Allow the paste to dry and your wallpapering is done.

    a PSQR   b SRQP
    c SQRP   d SRPQ

2. Taking a Photograph with a Digital Camera

A Find the 'on' button on top of the camera and press it. Wait for it to turn on and load.

P View your picture by using the playback button on the back of the camera.

Q Look into the LCD screen on the back of the camera to aim the camera at whatever your target is. Zoom in or out if necessary.

R Find the photo button (always on top right of the camera). Once the target is in the screen the way you want it, hold the camera still, press and hold the button until the camera flashes.

S Adjust settings if necessary (refer to users manual).

Z Attach a USB cord to your computer and upload your pictures onto your computer to print or save.

    a PSQR   b SQRP
    c PQRS   d SRQP

3. Cultivating a Crop

A Determine what crops you can raise in your location, depending on climate and rainfall. Accordingly, purchase the seeds required.

P Deweed your crops when the ground becomes packed by rainfall, or weeds become a problem. You may apply mulch to reduce or eliminate weed growth.

Q Watch for insects and animals which may damage your plants. You may have to resort to use of pesticides.

R Mark out the area you intend to plant, and with a hoe or plow, create a slightly raised bed in the loose soil in a line across the length of the plot. Next, make the furrow with a plough. Plant your seeds in the furrow at the depth required for the particular crop you are planting.

ENGLISH **OLYMPIAD** CLASS VIII

S   Break the ground by loosening the soil, and 'turning under', or covering, the plants or plant residue from a previous crop. This is referred to as 'tilling'.

Z   Harvest the crop when it is ripe.

    a PSQR   b SQRP   c SRPQ   d PQRS

4. Opening a Bank Account

A   Decide the kind of account you want to open - Savings, Current, FD, RD, etc.

P   Attach all the necessary documents to the form, hand it over to the dealing assistant and wait for confirmation about the opening of the account.

Q   Ask the dealing assistant for the relevant Account Opening Form and fill it up completely.

R   After confirmation is given, go to the Deposit counter and deposit the initial amount.

S   Go to the Bank branch convenient for you, carrying Identity Proof, Residence Proof and any other document required for opening the account. Carry sufficient money to make the initial deposit.

Z   Obtain the receipt for the deposit of the initial amount. Your account has been opened.

    a PQRS   b SRQP   c SQPR   d SRPQ

5. Life Cycle of a Butterfly

A   The female butterflies lay their eggs on plants after the mating period.

P   The caterpillar spends most of its time eating the plant.

Q   Most of the transformation takes place inside the pupa.

R   The caterpillar emerges from the egg after a few days.

S   The caterpillar forms a protection shield called 'pupa' when it has finished growing and is ready for transformation.

Z   When it has been transformed into a butterfly, it emerges from the pupa and flies away.

    a RPSQ   b SRQP
    c RSQP   d RPQS

Logical Sequencing in a Story

Judging the logic of the completion of a story means sequencing the given sentences in a logical way, so that the story is logically completed. In such kind of questions, the first and last sentences are identified and the remaining four sentences have to be arranged in order so that the story is logically completed.

Example

The story given below is divided into six parts with the first and last parts identified as A and Z. The remaining four parts of the story are labelled as P, Q, R and S. Find the correct sequence of these four parts and select the correct option accordingly.

A   After the vacations, Farida was excited about attending her first day in the new class at school.

P   After brushing her teeth, she set the alarm for 6:00 AM and climbed into bed.

Q   She left a note for her mother to pack tomato sandwiches for lunch at school.

R   The night before, she ironed her school uniform and laid it on a chair in her room.

S   In her school bag, she placed her new pencil box with markers, crayons and pencils.

Z   Farida lay for an hour wondering about the next day. Finally, her eyes shut and she fell asleep with a smile on her face.

    a RPSQ   b SRQP   c RSQP   d RPQS

Ans. *c*

Out of the four options given, this is the only one possible.

Practice Centre

In the given questions, the first and last sententences are identified and you have to arrange the middle order of the sentences.

1. A Last Saturday, Nalini and Kamal walked to their Nani's house nearby.

P While crossing through the park, Kamal picked some roses for Nani.

Q They jumped over a fence and left the park. Nalini waved hello to Mr. Sharif and helped him catch his newspaper, which the wind had blown away.

R On the way, they stopped by the fruit shop and bought an apple each, and ate them as they walked.

S Finally, Nalini and Kamal arrived at Nani's house.

Z She came out and welcomed them both a warm embrace.

a PQRS	b RQPS
c RPSQ	d RPQS

2. A A village boy had a very bad temper and got angry easily. So his father gave him a box of nails and a hammer, telling him to hammer one nail into a nearby wooden fence, every time he became angry.

P When he told this to his father, the father asked him to pull out one nail for each day that he was able to hold his temper. After some weeks, the boy reported to his father that now there were no nails in the fence any longer.

Q He had realised that it was easier to hold his temper than hammering the nails. Finally, one day he didn't get angry at all.

R The father took his son again to the fence, saying, "You have controlled your temper now, but look at the holes in the fence. It will never be the same again."

S On the first day, the boy had hammered 10 nails in the fence. However, over the following days the boy started controlling his anger and the number of nails in the fence reduced.

Z "Similarly, when you say something in anger, it leaves a scar like the ones in the fence. A verbal wound is as bad as a physical wound."

a SQPR	b SRQP
c SQRP	d PQRS

3. A Best friends Ramesh and Suresh were arguing while taking a walk along a fast flowing river in the hills of Uttarakhand. Enraged by a remark by Suresh, Ramesh gave him a tight slap on his cheek.

P Ramesh, seeing his friend's plight, ran down the river, caught Suresh's hand and pulled him out of the river to safety.

Q Suresh was hurt, but instead of saying something, took a twig and wrote on the river sand, "Today my best friend slapped me."

R After recovering, Suresh used a stone to write on a rock nearby, "Today my best friend saved my life." Ramesh was puzzled by this and asked Suresh, "Earlier, when I hurt you, you wrote on the sand, but now you write on a rock. Why?"

S After sometime, Suresh was tired and felt like bathing in the river. As soon as he stepped in, the strong current swept him away.

Z Suresh replied, "When anyone hurts us, we should write it on sand so that the winds or currents of forgiveness will erase it very soon. However, if somebody does something good for us, we should engrave it in stone where no current or wind will erase it."

a PSQR	b SRQP
c QSPR	d QRPS

4. A Tansen showed no interest in music while growing up.

P As they drew near, Tansen took a deep breath and let out a loud roar.

Q The people, thinking a lion was nearby, threw down their belongings and ran for their lives.

R One day, while he was sitting on a tree, chirping like the sparrows, he saw some travellers crossing the forest.

S Instead, he liked to spend his time in the forest, chasing animals and imitating their sounds.

Z However, when they heard a young boy laughing at their terror, they realised they have been fooled and shook their fists at him.

a PSQR	b SRQP
c PQRS	d SRPQ

ENGLISH **OLYMPIAD** CLASS VIII

5. A Mother Teresa was born Agnes Gonxha Bojaxhiu in Skopje, in Albania, then Yugoslavia, on August 27, 1910.

P "It is a missionary country like the countries of Africa", she explained when asked why she had chosen India.

Q As a 12 years old, she decided to become a nun, and at 18, she joined the Order of Loreto nuns in Ireland.

R There in that distant land, she would get the call to go to India.

S On joining the Order, Agnes took on the name 'Teresa'.

Z And it was in Calcutta that she arrived in 1929, to become a teacher in a Loreto school.

a PSQR	b QSRP
c PQSR	d SRPQ

Jumbled Sentence

Rearrangement of parts of a sentence to form a sentence having a logical meaning is one of the most common questions asked in an English language exam. It is neither based on any particular logic nor does it follow from any previously learnt concepts.

A sentence is a group of words making complete sense and ending in either a period (.), exclamation mark (!) or question mark (?), depending on whether it is an assertive, exclamatory or interrogative sentence respectively.

Every sentence has two parts, a subject and a predicate. The subject is a word / group of words that denotes someone or something about which something is said in the sentence. The predicate may be a word / group of words that informs what is said about the subject. The subject will be a noun or noun-equivalent phrase / clause. The predicate must contain a finite verb, either expressed or understood.

An example of a Multiple Choice Question on a jumbled sentence is given below.

Example *Arrange the four parts of the sentence given below in the correct order to make a meaningful sentence and select the correct option accordingly.*

A but also robbed him

B the thief not only

C of all his cash

D beat Mr Kapur black and blue,

a BDCA	b DCBA	c CABD	d BDAC

Answer (d)

Practice Centre

In each of the following questions, arrange the four parts of the sentence given below in the correct order to make a meaningful sentence and select the correct option accordingly.

1. A big heavy books

B I can't carry

C it's too full of

D this box because

a BADC	b CBDA
c BDCA	d ADBC

2. A their

B small neighbourhood

C all loved

D they

a DBCA	b DCAB
c ABCD	d ABDC

3. A reception before 11 AM

B the keys deposited at

C rooms must

D be vacated and

a CDBA	b BADC
c BCDA	d DCBA

4. A was offered

B to his

C a reward

D amazement, he

a ACDB	b BDCA
c CDAB	d BDAC

5. A do your
    B the evening
    C television in
    D parents watch
      a ADBC   **b** CBDA
      c DCBA   **d** ADCB

6. A when will
    B birthday present
    C you give
    D Manvendra his
      a BCAD   **b** CDBA
      c CDAB   **d** ACDB

7. A 8 o'clock bus
    B on Monday mornings
    C Jagdish always
    D takes the
      a CABD   **b** CDAB
      c BCAD   **d** ABDC

8. A in the world
    B be done to
    C something must
    D reduce poverty
      a ACDB   **b** CBAD
      c CBDA   **d** DBAC

9. A you please bring
    B the bread to
    C the dining room
    D Bindiya, could
      a DCBA   **b** ABCD
      c DABC   **d** BCAD

10. A the Japanese language
     B a lot of
     C characters in
     D there are
      a DBCA   **b** ADCB   **c** BCDA   **d** CADB

11. A he was asked
     B he answered
     C satisfactorily
     D many questions, which
      a ABDC   **b** DBAC   **c** DABC   **d** ADBC

12. A becomes necessary to
     B of the plan starts, it
     C once the implementation
     D evaluate performance
      a BACD   **b** CBAD
      c DBCA   **d** ADBC

13. A and have dinner
     B would you like
     C to come
     D with us tomorrow
      a DCBA   **b** ADBC
      c BCAD   **d** ABCD

14. A likes to go shopping
     B is in Gurgaon, she
     C with her friends
     D when Mrs Agrawal
      a DCBA   **b** BCAD
      c DBAC   **d** DABC

15. A of your life is
     B determined by the quality
     C the quality
     D of your thoughts
      a CABD   **b** CDBA
      c BDAC   **d** ADBC

16. A there are many
     B interesting books at
     C you read them all
     D the library; have
      a ABDC   **b** BACD
      c DBCA   **d** CDBA

17. A subordinates under him
     B a manager
     C motivate and guide the
     D should be able to
      a BCDA   **b** ACBD
      c DBAC   **d** BDCA

18. A stamps for her on
     B his way back from school
     C Mrs Sharma asked
     D him to buy some postage
      a ABDC   **b** DCAB
      c BACD   **d** CDAB

19. A really hard
     B but she works
     C earn much
     D Jaya doesn't
      a DCAB   **b** DCBA   **c** BADC   **d** CDAB

20. A there is no
     B point in
     C protesting against
     D the new law
      a CDAB   **b** DCBA
      c ABCD   **d** ABDC

10

Transformation of Sentences

Transformation is changing the form of a sentence without changing its meaning.

Types of Sentence Transformation

1. An interrogative sentence can be transformed into an assertive sentence and vice-versa without changing its meaning.

> ***Example 1*** When can their glory fade? *(interrogative sentence)*
> Their glory can never fade. *(assertive sentence)*

> ***Example 2*** We were not sent to this world simply to make money. *(assertive sentence)*
> Were we sent to this world simply to make money? *(interrogative sentence)*

2. An exclamatory sentence can be transformed into an assertive sentence and vice-versa without changing its meaning.

> ***Example 1*** How sweetly the moonlight sleeps upon the river-bank! *(exclamatory sentence)*
> The moonlight sweetly sleeps upon the river-bank. *(assertive sentence)*

> > ***Note:*** *Although such an exclamatory sentence can be transformed into an assertive sentence, an exclamatory sentence is preferred on many occasions to an assertive sentence for the emotional effect that the exclamatory sentence carries.*

> ***Example 2*** This sun is very hot. *(assertive sentence)*
> How hot the sun is! *(exclamatory sentence)*

3. One part of a sentence can be changed into another part of speech without changing the meaning.

(a) The verb of a sentence itself can be changed into another verb / its noun form without change in the meaning of the sentence.

> ***Example 1*** *The verb of a sentence itself can be changed into another verb.*
> This kind of joke never amuses me.
> This kind of joke never gives me any amusement.
> > *(the verb amuses has been changed into gives)*

> ***Example 2*** *The verb of a sentence can be changed into its noun form.*
> It costs twelve dollars.
> Its cost is twelve dollars. *(the verb costs has been changed into its noun form-cost)*

(b) An adjective can be changed into an adverb and vice-versa without change in the meaning of the sentence.

> ***Example 1*** *Adjective changed to adverb*
> He is a disgrace to his family. (the word *disgrace* is an adjective)
> He has disgraced his family. (the word *disgraced* is an adverb)

Example 2 *Adverb changed to adjective*

He replied curtly. (the word *curtly* is an adverb)

He gave a curt reply. (the word *curt* is an adjective)

(c) An adjective can be changed into its noun form and vice-versa without change in the meaning of the sentence.

Example 1 *Adjective changed to noun*

Mayank was not of any help in solving the problem. (the word *help* is an adjective)

Mayank was not helpful in solving the problem. (the word *helpful* is a noun)

Example 2 *Noun changed to adjective*

This matter is of no importance to me. (the word *importance* is a noun)

This matter is not important to me. (the word *important* is an adjective)

4. A clause in a sentence can be reduced to a phrase without changing the meaning of the sentence. Here three cases of this transformation will covered.

Case 1 Adjective clauses can be changed into to adjective phrases and vice–versa.

Example Dr Banerjee, who is the President of the university, will give a speech at the convocation.

The President of the university, Dr Banerjee, will give a speech at the convocation.

(the clause *who is the President of the university* has been changed to the phrase *The President of the university*.)

Case 2 Adverb clauses can be changed into adverb phrases and vice-versa.

Example As he was unsure of himself, the correct answer stuck in Sameer's throat.

Being unsure of himself, the correct answer stuck in Sameer's throat.

(the clause *As he was unsure of himself* has been changed to the phrase *Being unsure of himself*.)

Case 3 Noun clauses can be changed into noun phrases and vice–versa.

Example I don't know where I should turn for help.

I don't know where to turn for help.

(the clause *I should turn for help* has been changed to the phrase *to turn for help*.)

5. Conversion between Simple / Complex / Compound sentences.

Sentences can be grouped according to the presence of main clauses and subordinate clauses as follows

- Simple sentences, which have only one main clause.
- Complex sentences, which have one main clause and at least one subordinate clause. Subordinate clauses are introduced by conjunctions like *because, as, if, when, where, since* and *though*.
- Compound sentences, which have more than one main clause and no subordinate clauses. The conjunctions commonly used in compound sentences are *and, or, but, yet* and *for*.

Example 1 *Conversion of a simple sentence into a complex sentence*

I won the tournament, managing to shock everybody. (*simple sentence*)

When I won the tournament, I managed to shock everybody. (*complex sentence*)

Example 2 *Conversion of a complex sentence into a compound sentence*

Although Kavita is rich, she is not happy. (*complex sentence*)

Kavita is rich but she is not happy. (*compound sentence*)

Practice Centre

Exercise I

Transform the following Interrogative Sentences into Assertive Sentences by selecting the correct option.

1. Can anybody bear such an insult?
   a Nobody can bear such an insult.
   b Who will bear such an insult?
   c Anyone can bear such an insult.
   d There is no one who can bear such an insult.

2. Isn't health more precious than wealth?
   a Wealth is less precious than health.
   b Health is more precious than wealth.
   c Health is always precious.
   d There is nothing more precious than health.

3. Can't you work harder?
   a You can work harder.
   b You may work harder.
   c You should work harder.
   d You must work harder.

4. Will you please keep quiet?
   a You are requested to keep quiet.
   b Please keep quiet.
   c You must keep quiet.
   d You should keep quiet.

5. Isn't Javed taller than his brother?
   a Javed's brother is not taller than Javed.
   b Javed is taller than his brother.
   c Javed can be taller than his brother.
   d Javed may be taller than his brother.

6. Will we ever forget the good old days?
   a We will never forget the good old days.
   b Good old days will always be remembered.
   c We will always remember good old days.
   d Good old days are to be cherished always.

7. Haven't I done enough for you?
   a I have done quite a lot for you.
   b Much I have done for you.
   c I have done enough for you.
   d I have done much for you.

8. Will you please have something to drink?
   a Please have something to drink.
   b You should have something to drink.
   c You must drink something.
   d Please drink something.

9. Will you open the door, please?
   a Please open the door.
   b You are requested to open the door.
   c It will be better if you open the door.
   d You better open the door.

10. Didn't they enjoy themselves at the party?
    a They enjoyed quiet a lot at the party.
    b They enjoyed themselves at the party.
    c They enjoyed thoroughly at the party.
    d They enjoyed too much at the party.

Exercise II

Transform the following Assertive Sentences into Interrogative Sentences by selecting the correct option.

1. He was a villain to do such a deed.
   a Was he not a villain to do such a deed?
   b Was he not doing a villain type behaviour?
   c Was he not a villain to behave this way?
   d Was he a villain to behave this way?

2. No one can fall into the drain without getting dirty.
   a Who will not get dirty if one falls into the drain?
   b Who can fall into the drain without getting dirty?
   c Who can fall into the drain and not get dirty?
   d Who will fall into the drain and not get dirty?

3. This is not the kind of dress to be worn for a formal school function.
   a Is this the kind of dress to be worn for a formal school function?
   b Is this the dress you should wear for a formal school function?
   c Is this the kind of dress you have selected to wear at a formal school function?
   d Is this the kind of dress you want to wear for a formal school function?

4. I shall never forget those happy days.
   a Will I not remember ever those happy days?
   b Will I ever forget those happy days?
   c Shall I ever forget those happy days?
   d Should I ever forget those happy days?

5. Move your bicycle out of the way.
   a Can you move your bicycle out of the way?
   b Will you move your bicycle out of the way?
   c Can this bicycle be removed out of the way?
   d Is it possible to remove this bicycle out of the way?

6. Please hurry up and finish your dinner.
   a Will you hurry up and finish your dinner, please?
   b Will you finish your dinner while hurrying up?
   c Will you please finish your dinner?
   d Hurry up please and finish your dinner.

7. Stop talking and let me get some sleep.
   a May I got some sleep if you can stop talking.
   b Will you stop talking and let me get some sleep?
   c Can you stop talking and let me get some sleep?
   d Could you stop talking and let me get some sleep?

8. Please wait for me.
   a Will you please wait for me?
   b Will you wait for me, please?
   c Will you not wait for me, please?
   d Can you not wait for me please?

9. Let us have dinner at the pizza parlour.
   a Should we have dinner at the pizza parlour?
   b Should we meet at the pizza parlour to have dinner?
   c Should we all go to pizza parlour for dinner?
   d May we have dinner at pizza parlour.

10. Please climb on the chair to clean the ceiling fan.
   a Will you climb on the chair to clean the ceiling fan, please?
   b Will you clean the ceiling fan standing on the chair, please?
   c Will you get a chair and clean the ceiling fan, please?
   d Could you please climb on the chair to clean the ceiling fan?

Exercise III

Transform the following Exclamatory Sentences into Assertive Sentences by selecting the correct option.

1. If only I were young again!
   a I wish I was young again.
   b I wish I were young again.

2. What a delicious meal this is!
   a The meal is delicious.
   b Delicious this meal is.

3. What a beautiful flower this is!
   a This is a beautiful flower.
   b It is a very beautiful flower.

4. What a great victory it was!
   a A great victory it was really.
   b It was a great victory.

5. How kind of you to help him at this difficult time!
   a It is very kind of you to help him at this difficult time.
   b It is a very difficult time; it is very kind of you to help him.

6. What a glorious morning last Sunday was!
   a It was indeed a glorious morning last Sunday.
   b Last Sunday every one experienced a glorious morning.

7. How clever that thief was to elude his captors!
   a The thief was very clever to elude his captors!
   b The thief was clever enough to elude his captors.

8. How noble he is!
   a He is nearly noble.
   b He is truly noble.

9. What a pleasant surprise this is!
   a This is indeed a pleasant surprise.
   b It is a very pleasant surprise.

10. How foolish it was of him to abuse the Chairman!
   a He was foolish to abuse the Chairman.
   b It was foolish of him to abuse the Chairman.

Exercise IV

Transform the following Assertive Sentences into Exclamatory Sentences by selecting the correct option.

1. It was an extremely delightful party.
   - a What a party! extremely delightful!
   - b What an extremely delightful party it was!

2. These children are really exceptional.
   - a How exceptional these children really are!
   - b What exceptional children these are!

3. You are brilliant, as you solved the puzzle.
   - a Very brilliant! you solved the puzzle!
   - b Brilliant, you solved the puzzle!

4. You are very boring.
   - a How boring you are!
   - b How boring of you!

5. She is a very nice person.
   - a What a nice person she is!
   - b How nice of her!

6. It's a challenge to teach so many gifted children.
   - a How challenging to teach so many gifted children!
   - b What a challenge it is to teach so many gifted children!

7. He's a very demanding boss.
   - a He is such a demanding boss!
   - b How demanding such a boss is!

8. She is a very ignorant person.
   - a What an ignorant person she is!
   - b How ignorant she is!

9. He's a compulsive video games addict.
   - a He is such a video game addict!
   - b What a compulsive video game addict he is!

10. This landscape is very marvellous.
    - a What a marvellous landscape this is!
    - b How marvellous this landscape is!

Exercise V

Transform the main verb of the following sentences into its noun form without changing the meaning of the sentences by selecting the correct option to fill in the blank.

1. You may explain your bad behaviour in the class party.

   Give the ______ for your bad behaviour in the class party.
   - a explain
   - b explanation
   - c explaining
   - d explained

2. Nobody can understand why you refused to lead the team.

   Nobody can understand your ______ to lead the team.
   - a refutal
   - b refusal
   - c refuse
   - d refusing

3. The two teams agreed to call off the match. There was an ______ between the two teams to call off the match.
   - a agreement
   - b agreeing
   - c agree
   - d agreed

4. Sudhanshu did not invite many of his family members for his birthday party.

   Sudhanshu did not send an ______ to many of his family members for his birthday party.
   - a invite
   - b invited
   - c invitation
   - d inviting

5. You must offer a bouquet of flowers to your teacher on Teacher's Day.

   ______ a bouquet of flowers to your teacher is necessary on Teacher's Day.
   - a Offering
   - b Offerings
   - c Offered
   - d Offer

6. Rashid should not compare his height with Karim, because he is too short.

   Rashid should not make a ______ of his height with Karim, because he is too short.
   - a comparement
   - b comparison
   - c compared
   - d comparing

7. It will be incorrect for you to believe that Ashok is honest, as he always tells lies.

   As Ashok always tells lies, you ______ that Ashok is honest is incorrect.
   - a believed
   - b believing
   - c belief
   - d believe

8. The teacher must permit students to go home early when there is heavy rain.

   The teacher must give ______ to students to go home early when there is heavy rain.
   - a permittance
   - b permitted
   - c permission
   - d permit

9. He begged me to forgive him for the treachery he had committed.

He begged _______ from me for the treachery he had committed.

a forgiveness   b forgivance
c forgiving   d forgive

10. Ramesh did not complain about the bad food because of his timid nature.

Ramesh did not register his _______ about the bad food because of his timid nature.

a comply   b complaint
c complained   d complaining

Exercise VI

Choose the correct adverb to fill in the blanks given below.

1. Sameer thought about the matter _______ .
   a careful   b carefulness
   c carefully   d carefulment

2. Rajat _______ began to understand.
   a gradual   b gradually
   c gradualness   d gradualfull

3. Can't you speak more _______ ?
   a quietness   b quiet
   c quietly   d quietfully

4. Lalit _______ accepted the offer.
   a happily   b happiness
   c happy   d happinessfully

5. My brother walks very _______ .
   a quickness   b quickly
   c quickment   d quickfully

6. I _______ understand what you're saying.
   a completely   b completeness
   c completement   d complete

7. This incident changed the situation _______ .
   a dramatic section   b dramatically
   c dramatic   d dramatised

8. Parveen reacted _______ to the announcement.
   a favourableness   b favourably
   c favourable   d favourful

9. Savita speaks very _______ .
   a fastness   b fast
   c fastly   d fastfully

10. The little baby fell very _______ .
    a bad   b badly
    c worse   d badfully

Exercise VII

Choose the correct noun to fill in the blanks in the following sentences from the options given.

1. Lalit showed enormous ___ when he gave part of his inheritance to charity.
   a generousness   b generosity
   c generous   d generous nature

2. It's Fazal's ___ to postpone the meeting.
   a responsibleness   b responsible
   c responsibility   d response

3. We must respect Tanvi's ___ of speech.
   a freeness   b freedom
   c free   d sense of freedom

4. Kavita's ___ was noticed by the Principal.
   a brilliance   b brilliantness
   c brilliant   d brightness

5. We were really pleased with the ___ of his welcome.
   a warmness   b warmth
   c warm   d warmfulness

6. He recovered ___ an hour after the accident.
   a consciousness   b consciously
   c conscious   d conscience

7. Crime and ___ can't be controlled in big cities.
   a violentness   b violence
   c violent   d violent behaviour

8. All men should be treated with ___ .
   a justly   b justice
   c just   d justiceness

9. Never underestimate the ___ of your ancestors.
   a wisdom   b wiseness
   c wise   d wisefulness

10. I feel like a ___ in this city.
    a strangeness   b stranger
    c strange   d strangement

ENGLISH **OLYMPIAD** CLASS VIII

Exercise VIII

Transform the adjective / adverb / noun clauses in the following sentences into phrases without changing the meaning of the sentences by selecting the correct option to fill in the blank.

1. There is no end to the problems that face a head of state.

   The problems faced by a head of state are ______.

   a unending   b too many   c too big   d enormous

2. The photographs which were published in the newspaper were extraordinary.

   The photographs published in the newspaper were ______

   a ordinary   b extraordinary   c exceptional   d exceptionally

3. The psychologists who study the nature of sleep have made important discoveries.

   Psychologists ______ the nature of sleep have made important discoveries.

   a studied   b having studies   c studying   d study

4. Kuala Lumpur, which is the capital of Malaysia, is a major trade centre in South-East Asia.

   Kuala Lumpur, ______ of Malaysia, is a major trade center in Southeast Asia.

   a the capital city
   b the capital
   c the capitalist
   d capital city

5. Two out of three people who are struck by lightning survive.

   Two out of three people ______ by lightning survive.

   a strike   b struck   c stricker   d stricken

6. When Suresh heard the sound of the engine, he realised that the car had started.

   ______ the sound of the engine, Suresh realised that the car had started.

   a Having heard   b Heard   c Hearing   d Hear

7. After Dr Bell had successfully tested the new apparatus again and again, he confidently announced the invention of the telephone to the world.

   After ______ the new apparatus again and again, Dr Bell confidently announced the invention of the telephone to the world.

   a successfully testing
   b having successfully tested
   c tested
   d testing

8. Because many people believe that wolves kill human beings, they fear them.

   ______ that wolves kill human beings, many people fear them.

   a The belief   b Believed   c Believing   d Having believed

Exercise IX

Fill in the blanks in the transformed sentences by choosing the best option.

1. At the time of serving dinner, there was a knock at the door.

   ______ there was a knock at the door.

   a As I was serving dinner
   b While I was serving dinner
   c Serving dinner
   d Just when serving dinner

2. That night Karan had a dream like a nightmare.

   That night Karan had a dream, ______ a nightmare.

   a that was more like   b which was more like   c it was more like   d that was unlike

3. Blinded by a dust storm, they lost their way.

   ______ by a dust storm, they lost their way.

   a Since they were blinded
   b As they were blinded
   c Being blinded
   d Because of being blinded

4. Non–vegetarians are not allowed to enter into the temple.

   ______, you can't be allowed to enter into the temple.

   a You being a non-vegetarian
   b If you are a non-vegetarian
   c As you are a non-vegetarian
   d If, a non-vegetarian

5. Brave people never lose courage.

People _____ never lose courage.

   a who are brave

   b that are brave

   c with bravery

   d those are brave

6. Though Salman is brave, he is careless.

Salman is brave _____

   a though careless

   b but careless

   c yet careless

   d still careless

7. Walk carefully lest you fall.

Walk carefully _____.

   a or you will fall   b but you will fall

   c otherwise you will fall   d otherwise will you fall

8. As soon as the soldiers heard the gunshots they rushed to the spot.

The soldiers heard the gunshots _____ to the spot.

   a rushed

   b and immediately rushed

   c rushing immediately

   d and rush

Exercise X

Each sentence / sentence group given below contains an underlined part. From the given options, choose the one that will correctly replace the underlined part and make the sentence grammatically correct.

1. The cheetah can run faster than the antelope. It is the speediest of the two.

   a the most speedier

   b the speedier

   c more speedy

   d No improvement required

2. We do not know where Vasudev was educated or what did he do to earn a living because history is silent about his early life.

   a what he did

   b what he had done

   c what had he done

   d No improvement required

3. You have been working very hard for many years, didn't you?

   a haven't you?

   b weren't you?

   c hadn't you?

   d No improvement required

4. He asked me did you forget to bring your raincoat.

   a did I forget to bring my raincoat?

   b if I forgot to bring my raincoat.

   c if I had forgotten to bring my raincoat.

   d No improvement required

5. Having learned that there was a vacancy for a computer operator, an application was submitted by me.

   a an application has been submitted by me

   b an application by me was submitted

   c I submitted an application

   d No improvement required

6. Be sure to contact with as many teachers as possible.

   a contact

   b contact to

   c contact on

   d No improvement required

7. This is the first time that the river Ganga has overflown its banks at Haridwar.

   a overflew

   b overflowed

   c has overflowed

   d No improvement required

8. Priyanka gave her daughter a children's colourfully illustrated encyclopedia.

   a a child's colourfully illustrated encyclopedia

   b a colourfully illustrated children's encyclopedia

   c an illustrated children's colourful encyclopedia

   d No improvement required

9. Sarvesh congratulated me for my winning the first prize in the class.

   a on my winning

   b at my winning

   c in my winning

   d No improvement required

10. I hope it will not rain when they have started their journey.

   a they will have started their journey

   b they will start their journey

   c they start their journey

   d No improvement required

Direct and Reported Speech

Reported speech (also called indirect speech) is when you tell somebody else what you or a person said before. Distinction must be made between direct speech and reported speech. When we use reported speech, we report either statements, questions, requests / commands or other types of sentences.

Types of Reported Speech

1. **When transforming statements** We should check whether we have to change *pronouns*, the *tense* or the *place, demonstratives* and *time expression*.

   * In reported speech, we often have to change the pronoun depending on who says what.

     Example   She says, "My dad likes roast chicken." *will change to*
     She says that her dad likes roast chicken.

   * If the sentence starts in the present, there is no change of tense in reported speech. However, if the sentence starts in the past, there is often change of tense (shifting back) in reported speech.

     Example   He says, "I write English poems." *will be changed to*
     He says that he writes English poems.
     (*No change in tense*)

     but   He said, "I am happy." *will be changed to*
     He said that he was happy.
     (*Tense is changed or shifted back*)

   * Place, demonstratives and time expressions change if the context of the reported statement (i.e. the location and/or the period of time) is different from that of the direct speech.
     - Place   *Here* is changed to *there.*
     - Demonstratives   *This* is changed to *that.*
     These is changed to *those.*

   * Time expressions change as (some examples)

Direct Speech	Reported Speech
today	that day
now	then
yesterday	the day before
days ago	days before
last week	the week before
next year	the following year
tomorrow	the next day / the following day

2. **When transforming questions** We should check whether we have to change *pronouns*, the *tense* or the *place, demonstratives* and *time expression.*

   In addition, to transform a direct question into an indirect question, we use question words (*where, when, what, how*) or if / whether, provided it is not there.

   Example   He said, "Why don't you speak English?" *will change to*
   He asked me why I didn't speak English.

   but   He said, "Do you speak English?" *will change to*
   He asked me whether / if I spoke English.

3. **When reporting requests/commands** We should check whether we have to change *pronouns* and *place* and *time expression*.

Example	He said, "Nancy, do the exercise." will change *to*
of command	He told Nancy to do the exercise.
Example	He said, "Nancy, please give me your pen." *will change to*
of request	He requested / asked Nancy to give him / her pen.

4. **When reporting other types of sentences** Some rules to be followed are:

- Expressions of advice with *must, should* and *ought* are usually reported using *advise / urge*.

  Example   He said, "You must read this book." *will change to*
  He advised / urged me to read that book.

- The expression *let's* is usually reported using *suggest*. In this case, there are two possibilities for reported speech, as given in the example below.

Example	He said, "Let's go to the cinema." *will change to*
either	He suggested going to the cinema.
or	He suggested that we should go to the cinema.

- If two complete main clauses are connected with *and, or, but, put, that* after the conjunction.

  Example   He said, "I saw her but she didn't see me." *will change to*
  He said that he had seen her but she hadn't seen him.

However, if the subject is not present (i.e. dropped) in the second main clause (the conjunction is directly followed by a verb), do not use *that*.

Example   She said, "I am a nurse and work in a hospital." *will change to*
She said that she was a nurse and worked in a hospital.

Practice Centre

Exercise I

Change the direct speech into reported speech by choosing the correct option.

1. Mohini said, "I visited my parents during the weekend."

Mohini said that she _______ her parents during the weekend.

  a has visited   **b** did visit
  c had visited   **d** visited

2. Girish said, "I didn't go to the party".
Girish said that he _______ to the party.

  a has gone   **b** had not gone
  c went   **d** will have gone

3. Malini said, "I hadn't travelled by the Metro train before I came to Delhi".

Malini said that she _______ by the Metro train before she _______ to Delhi.

  a did not travel, came
  b hadn't travelled, had come
  c hadn't travelled, came
  d never travelled, had come

4. She said, "He hasn't eaten breakfast."
She said/informed that he _______ .

  a didn't eat   **b** hadn't eaten
  c haven't eaten   **d** will not have eaten

5. Harish said, "We went out last night."
Harish informed that they _______ the previous night.

  a had gone out
  b have gone out
  c did go
  d has gone out

6. Raveena said, "I'm coming, wait for me"!
   Raveena exclaimed that we should wait for
   her, as she _______.
   a is coming   b was coming
   c has been coming   d had been coming

7. Arvind said, "I was waiting for the bus when
   Vinod arrived."
   Arvind said that he _______ for the bus
   when Vinod arrived.
   a has been waiting   b had been waiting
   c have been waiting d was waiting

8. Deepika said, "I was sleeping when Priya
   called."
   Deepika said that she _______ when Priya
   called.
   a was sleeping   b has been sleeping
   c had been sleeping   d were sleeping

9. He said, "They would help if they could."
   He said that they _______ if they could.
   a would have helped b would help
   c had helped   d will have helped

10. Dilip said, "I'd never been there before."
    Dilip said that he _______ before.
    a had never been there
    b would never had been there
    c could never had been there
    d has been there.

Exercise II

Change the direct sentence into reported speech by choosing the correct option.

1. She said, "He works in a bank."
   She said that he _______ in a bank.
   a had worked   b worked
   c has worked   d did work

2. He said, "We went out last night."
   He said that they _______ the night before.
   a have gone out b has gone out
   c had gone out   d went out

3. Leela said, "I am coming to the party."
   Leela said that she _______ to the party.
   a was coming   b has been coming
   c would be coming d will be coming

4. Priya said, "I was waiting for the bus when
   my dad arrived."
   Priya said that she _______ for the bus
   when her dad arrived.

a has been waiting   b had been waiting
c would be waiting   d was waiting

5. She said, "I had never been there before."
   She said that she _______ there before.
   a has never been   b had never been
   c have never been   d never went

6. Meera said, "He did not go to the party."
   Meera said that he _______ to the party.
   a has not gone   b never went
   c had not gone   d did not go

7. Jiten said, "I will eat pizza for dinner."
   Jiten said that he _______ pizza for dinner.
   a will   b will be eating
   c would eat   d is going to eat

8. She said, "I will finish my work by the
   weekend."
   She said that she _______ her work by the
   weekend.
   a had finished   b would have finished
   c would be finishing d would finish

9. She said, "It was already raining when she
   got here."
   She said that it _______ when she got there.
   a has been raining b had been raining
   c would be raining d rained

10. Paul said, "I have been on a holiday."
    Paul said that he _______ on a holiday.
    a had been   b has been
    c was   d was been

Exercise III

Change the reported commands and questions into direct speech by choosing the correct option.

1. He answered them that he would soon
   return.
   He answered them, "I _______ return."
   a shall soon   b will soon
   c would soon   d am soon going to

2. He told me that I might leave that place as
   soon as I could.
   He told me, "You _______ this place as soon
   as _______."
   a should leave, you should
   b may leave, you can
   c will leave, you would
   d may leave, you could

3. I admitted that I had acted foolishly in what I said.

   I admitted, "I _____ foolishly in what I said."
   - a have acted
   - b has acted
   - c acted
   - d had acted

4. He told them that he had been robbed of the book which he had brought.

   He said," I _____ of the book which I _____."
   - a have been robbed, bought
   - b has been robbed, buy
   - c had been robbed, buy
   - d had been robbed, bought

5. He said that he was sorry for the fault he had committed.

   He said,"I _____ for the fault I _____."
   - a am sorry, have committed
   - b was sorry, had committed
   - c will be sorry, had committed
   - d am sorry, had committed

6. They affirmed that he was the best worker they had seen.

   They affirmed,"He _____ worker we _____."
   - a are, had seen
   - b is the best, have seen
   - c is the best, has seen
   - d is the best, had seen

7. He admitted that he had not worked as hard as John had done.

   He admitted,"I _____ as hard as John has done."
   - a have not worked
   - b will have not worked
   - c not been working
   - d did not work

8. He heard them say that he did not deserve the prize.

   He heard them say,"He _____ the prize".
   - a had not deserved
   - b has not deserved
   - c does not deserve
   - d did not deserve

9. He made a promise that he would do it as soon as he could.

   He made a promise, "I _____ as soon as I _____."
   - a shall do it, could
   - b will do it, could
   - c will do it, can
   - d would do it, can

10. They said that he had deserved their thanks for all he had done.

    They said,"He _____ our thanks for all he has done."
    - a has deserved
    - b had deserved
    - c will deserve
    - d deserved

Exercise IV

Directions for Q. Nos. (1-14) *Read the dialogues and report correctly by filling in the blanks in the reported speech by selecting the correct option from those given below the reported speech.*

Ajay	"What are you doing here Asha? I haven't seen you since April."
Asha	"I've just come back from my two months long holiday in Kashmir."
Ajay	"Did you enjoy it?"
Asha	"I love Kashmir. And the Kashmiri people were so friendly."
Ajay	"Did you visit the Amarnath shrine?"
Asha	"Unfortunately, no. I can show you some pictures of Kashmir. Are you free tomorrow morning?"
Ajay	"I must arrange a couple of things. But I am free this evening."
Asha	"You can come to my place at seven. Is that all right?"
Ajay	"Okay."

Dialogues in Reported Speech

Ajay asked Asha **1.**_______. He further added that he **2.**_______. Asha explained that **3.**_______. Ajay wondered **4.**_______. Asha told him that she **5.**_______ and that **6.**_______. Ajay wanted to know **7.**_______. Asha said that **8.**_______ but that she **9.**_______. Then she asked him **10.**_______. Ajay explained that **11.**_______. But he added that **12.**_______. Asha suggested that **13.**_______ at seven and asked him **14.**_______. Ajay replied that it was fine.

Options

1.
   - a what she was doing there
   - b what was she doing there?
   - c what she has been doing there
   - d what she had been doing there

2.
   - a hasn't seen her since April
   - b didn't seen her since April
   - c hadn't seen her since April
   - d didn't see her since April

3.
   - a she has just come back from her two months long holiday in Kashmir
   - b she had just come back from her two months long holiday in Kashmir
   - c she just came back from her two months long holiday in Kashmir
   - d she was coming back from her two months long holiday in Kashmir

4.
   a if she enjoyed that
   b if she has enjoyed it
   c if she had enjoyed it
   d if she did enjoy that

5.
   a loves Kashmir
   b loved Kashmir
   c has loved Kashmir
   d had loved Kashmir

6.
   a and the Kashmir people have been so friendly
   b and the Kashmir people are so friendly
   c the Kashmiri people had been so friendly
   d the Kashmiri people were so friendly

7.
   a if she had visited the Amarnath Shrine
   b if she has visited the Amarnath Shrine
   c if she is visiting the Amarnath Shrine
   d if she did visit the Amarnath Shrine

8.
   a unfortunately, she hasn't
   b unfortunately she did not
   c unfortunately she could not
   d unfortunately she hadn't

9.
   a would show him some pictures of Kashmir
   b could show him some pictures of Kashmir
   c will show him some pictures of Kashmir
   d can show him some pictures of Kashmir

10.
   a if he was free the next morning
   b if he would be free the next morning
   c if he were free the next morning
   d if he will be free the next morning

11.
   a he must arrange a couple of things
   b he must have arranged a couple of things
   c he has to arrange a couple of things
   d he must be arranging a couple of things

12.
   a he was free that evening
   b he has been free that evening
   c he will be free that evening
   d he would be free that evening

13.
   a he has to come to her place
   b he should come to her place
   c he could come to her place
   d he could have come to her place

14.
   a if that was all right
   b if that will be all right
   c if that would be all right
   d if it was all right

Exercise V

Convert the sentences given below into reported speech, starting all your answers with 'He', and use the simple past of 'ask', 'say', 'request' or 'tell'.

Do not change the time expressions. Two examples are given below to guide you.

***Example* 1** "Could you give me the glass on the table, please?" - He requested me to give her the glass on the table.

***Example* 2** "Would you mind telling me how to get to the art gallery, please?"- He asked me how to get to the art gallery.

Select the correct option for each of the following.

1. "I usually drink coffee in the mornings."
   a He told that he usually drank coffee in the mornings.
   b He told that he usually has drunk coffee in the mornings.
   c He told that he usually drinks coffee in the morning.
   d He told that he usually has been drinking coffee in the morning.

2. "Come quickly!"
   a He asked to come quickly.
   b He asked me that he should come quickly.
   c He asked me to come quickly.
   d He asked me for coming quickly.

3. "They had never been to Mumbai until last year."
   a He told that they had never been to Mumbai until last year.
   b He told that they have never been to Mumbai until last year.
   c He said that they were never been to Mumbai until last year.
   d He told they never been to Mumbai until last year.

4. "Please don't forget my book."
   a He requested me not to forget his book.
   b He requested not to have forgotten his book.
   c He requested not forgetting his book.
   d He requested me not to forgot his book.

5. "Please buy bread on your way home."
   a He requested buying bread on my way home.
   b He requested me to buy bread on my way home.
   c He ordered me to buy a bread on my way home.
   d He requested me to have bought bread on my way home.

12 Cloze Test

Cloze tests require the ability to understand context and vocabulary in order to identify the correct words or type of words that belong to the deleted parts of a text. A Cloze Test is a procedure in which we are asked to supply words that have been removed from a passage as a test of our ability to understand the given text.

Example *Fill in the blanks in the passage given below by selecting the best option from those given below the passage.*

This morning, I went to the __________ **1.** and bought some milk and eggs. I knew it was going to rain, but I forgot to take my __________ **2.**, and ended up getting wet on the way __________ **3.**.

1. (a) market	(b) garage	(c) road	d. station
2. (a) shoes	(b) overcoat	(c) umbrella	d. gloves
3. (a) returning	(b) behind	(c) forward	d. back

Answers   1. (a)   2. (c)   3. d.

The first blank is preceded by "the"; therefore, a noun, an adjective or an adverb must follow. However, a conjunction follows the blank; the sentence would not be grammatically correct if anything other than a noun were in the blank. The words "milk and eggs" are important for deciding which noun to put in the blank; "supermarket" is a possible answer; depending on the student, however, the first blank could either be store, supermarket, shop or market, while umbrella or raincoat fits the second. In the third blank, 'returning' or 'behind' will be grammatically incorrect.

Types of Cloze Test

1. **Grammar Cloze**   Four major word classes tested in these are *determiners, pronouns, prepositions* and *connectors*.
2. **Vocabulary Cloze**   Here you have to apply your vocabulary skills and knowledge to answer multiple choice questions.
3. **Comprehension Cloze**   Here you have to come up with suitable words on your own to fill in the blanks.

Practice Centre

Exercise I Grammar Cloze

Directions   *Fill in each blank with the most suitable word from the box given above the passage. Each word can be used only once. The options given refer to the number of the word in the box.*

(i) a	(ii) and	(iii) as	(iv) for	(v) from
(vi) in	(vii) it	(viii) its	(ix) of	(x) or
(xi) that	(xii) the	(xiii) these	(xiv) those	(xv) with

The word 'Capsicum', originally from Central America, is the botanical name __________ **1.** a range of fruits (technically it is a fruit) __________ **2.** includes chillies, bell peppers and long banana peppers. __________ **3.** Singapore, the name 'capsicum' is used. In the USA __________ **4.** UK, the fruit is called 'bell pepper' __________ **5.** just 'pepper'.

__________ **6.** versatile (can be eaten raw or cooked) fruits come in all shapes and sizes. In terms __________ **7.** colour, capsicums range __________ **8.** green capsicums that turn red __________ **9.** they ripen, to __________ **10.** medley of orange, yellow, purple and black shades. Whatever __________ **11.** shape or colour, the bigger the fruit, the sweeter the taste; the smaller __________ **12.** fruit, the spicier __________ **13.** is. When choosing capsicums, go for __________ **14.** with glossy skins. Avoid the ones __________ **15.** soft spots or blemishes.

1. a (i)	b (ii)	c (iii)	d (iv)
2. a (xi)	b (iv)	c (iii)	d (x)
3. a (i)	b (vi)	c (iii)	d (iv)
4. a (i)	b (ii)	c (iii)	d (iv)
5. a (iii)	b (ii)	c (x)	d (iv)
6. a (xii)	b (ii)	c (xv)	d (xiii)
7. a (ix)	b (xii)	c (ii)	d (iv)
8. a (v)	b (ii)	c (iii)	d (iv)
9. a (vi)	b (ii)	c (iii)	d (iv)
10. a (vi)	b (vii)	c (i)	d (iv)
11. a (vi)	b (vii)	c (i)	d (viii)
12. a (vi)	b (xii)	c (xi)	d (xv)
13. a (vi)	b (vii)	c (i)	d (iv)
14. a (xvi)	b (xv)	c (ix)	d (xiv)
15. a (xv)	b (v)	c (xi)	d (xiii)

Exercise II Vocabulary Cloze

Directions *Replace each underlined word / phrase with the most suitable word from the options given below the passage.*

A few years ago, Ruth Weikfield, together with her husband, <u>converted</u> **1** an old toll tax barrier building which they had bought into a restaurant and lodging house. In earlier days, such buildings were places where motorists paid their road <u>tolls</u> **2**, ate some snacks and continued their journey.

One day Ruth decided to bake cookies for her guests, but she had <u>run out of</u> **3** baker's chocolate. She found a Nestle chocolate bar in the <u>pantry</u> **4**, broke it into pieces, and threw the pieces into the cookie batter, thinking that they would melt during baking. Instead, they <u>held</u> **5** their shape, and the chocolate chip cookie was born.

Soon Nestle noticed that its chocolate bar sales <u>jumped</u> **6** in the area where Ruth's inn was <u>located</u> **7** Nestle met up with Ruth and learnt more about her increasingly famous chocolate chip cookie. <u>Taking her suggestion on board</u> **8**, Nestle began <u>scoring</u> **9** their chocolate to allow for easier breaking. They also began printing Ruth's <u>recipe</u> **10** on the back of each chocolate pack.

1. a destroyed	b adapted	c rebuilt	d modified
2. a costs	b taxes	c amounts	d payments
3. a no more	b no useful	c not enough	d not broken
4. a kitchen	b refrigerator	c storeroom	d cupboard
5. a formed	b kept	c moulded	d earned
6. a hiked	b extended	c hopped	d increased
7. a situated	b pinpointed	c unearthed	d given
8. a Considering her suggestion		b Discussing her suggestion	
c Accepting her suggestion		d Exposing her suggestion	
9. a increasing	b numbering	c scratching	d recording
10. a cooking method	b prescription	c blueprint	d style

Exercise III Comprehension Cloze

Directions   *Fill in each blank with the most suitable word from the box given above the passage. Each word can be used only once. The options given refer to the number of the word in the box.*

(i) been	(ii) before	(iii) created	(iv) custody	(v) from	(vi) had	(vii) in
(viii) including	(ix) of	(x) officers	(xi) on	(xii) others	(xiii) out	
(xiv) suspect	(xv) suspects	(xvi) that	(xvii) to	(xviii) was	(xix) were	(xx) would

Two students from Shahdulganj, aged 17 and 18, are accused __________1. plotting an attack at their school on November 20, the first anniversary of the shooting at Sarvodaya School in Tarpapur, __________2. which 18-year old ex-student Karan Kalwant carried __________3., an attack __________4. left six people wounded by gunshots and __________5. wounded by detonated smoke bombs, __________6. taking his own life.

One of the __________7., aged 17, killed himself on Friday after a confrontation with a high school teacher and police __________8.. The plot __________9. uncovered when a school principal __________10. discovered a web page the 17-year-old suspect had __________11., showing material that glorified the two perpetrators of the Sarvodaya School massacre.

The second __________12., aged 18, is in police __________13., and has confessed __________14. the plot.

Materials __________15. two crossbows, two air guns, instructions __________16. how to build a pipe bomb and a list of potential victims had __________17. seized by Shahdulganj police when they __________18. alerted that the plot __________19. have taken place at the Shahdulganj public gymnasium. The items had been confiscated __________20. their homes.

1. a (ix) b (xii) c (xiii) d (xiv)
2. a (xvi) b (vii) c (viii) d (xi)
3. a (xi) b (xii) c (xiii) d (xiv)
4. a (xi) b (xii) c (xiii) d (xvi)
5. a (xvi) b (ix) c (xii) d (xiv)
6. a (ii) b (vi) c (iii) d (iv)
7. a (xi) b (xv) c (xiii) d (xiv)
8. a (xv) b (xii) c (xiii) d (x)
9. a (xviii) b (xii) c (ix) d (xiv)
10. a (viii) b (vi) c (xv) d (iv)
11. a (iii) b (i) c (xv) d (iv)
12. a (viii) b (vi) c (xv) d (xiv)
13. a (viii) b (vi) c (xv) d (iv)
14. a (xvii) b (vi) c (xv) d (iv)
15. a (viii) b (vi) c (xv) d (iv)
16. a (viii) b (vi) c (xv) d (xi)
17. a (viii) b (vi) c (i) d (iv)
18. a (viii) b (xix) c (xv) d (xx)
19. a (xx) b (xvi) c (xv) d (xiv)
20. a (xvii) b (vi) c (iv) d (v)

13 Spoken and Written Expressions

Exercise I

Complete each gap with a suitable word from the options given below the passage.

Teacher to students: "I'm afraid I haven't got enough copies of this exercise. I tried to have more run _________ **1.** but the photocopier had broken _________ **2.** and the repairman didn't turn _________ **3.** when he was supposed to. He did ring _________ **4.** to say he'd been held _________ **5.** unexpectedly, but that's the second time that company has let us _________ **6.** recently. Well, there's nothing else for it: you're just going to have to look _________ **7.** with your neighbour. While you're doing that, I'll just give _________ **8.** the test you did last week. Some of you slipped _________ **9.** in a few places, but, on the whole, the results were good. If you carry _________ **10.** as you've been doing, you should do fine!"

1.	a down	b off	c up	d in
2.	a up	b away	c down	d at
3.	a down	b away	c up	d off
4.	a up	b on	c down	d at
5.	a on	b up	c down	d in
6.	a down	b up	c away	d of
7.	a upon	b on	c up	d at
8.	a up	b back	c away	d off
9.	a upon	b up	c down	d in
10.	a on		b up	
	c along		d of	

Exercise II

Complete each sentence with a suitable word from the given options.

1. We spent more last month than we earned, so we're in the ________ again.
   a green b black c red d blue

2. Those campers are really ________, as they have no idea how to set up a tent.
   a white b green c blue d red

3. The baby screamed ________ murder when his naughty sister took his toys away.
   a red b black c blue d white

4. The thief was caught ________- handed, as he was robbing the bank when the police arrived.
   a blue b red c green d purple

5. Sonia had no idea she was going to lose her job; the news came out of the ________.
   a red b green c blue d white

6. Kishore has ________ fingers, because everything grows well in his garden.
   a green b blue c yellow d red

7. Our exams are over and it's time to celebrate; so we're going to paint the town ________.
   a green b red c blue d white

8. We go to restaurants once in a ________ moon, as the last time was some years ago.
   a blue b red c green d white

9. Guru's mother saw ________ when he told her he'd sold their cow for a sackful of grain.
   a green b blue c black d red

10. If he'd used his little ________ cells, he'd have realised it was a stupid thing to do.
    a black b grey c blue d red

Exercise III

Complete each sentence with a suitable word from the options given. In all the sentences, options have been given.

1. Her eyes are ______, like the colour of the sky.
   - a red
   - b blue
   - c grey

2. He was in a hurry so he ______ a taxi to the station.
   - a brought
   - b made
   - c took

3. I'm half French: my mother is English but my ______ was born in Paris.
   - a brother
   - b sister
   - c father

4. Romeo and Juliet was ______ by William Shakespeare.
   - a wrote
   - b written
   - c write

5. Everest is the highest ______ in the world.
   - a hill
   - b mountainous
   - c mountain

6. "Excuse me, would you mind if I ______ down here?"
   - a sit
   - b sat
   - c seat

7. He can't open the door because it's ______ and he's lost his key.
   - a lock
   - b bolted
   - c locked

8. My ______ are not as good as they were; I think I need glasses.
   - a glasses
   - b lens
   - c eyes

9. The Olympic ______ are held every four years.
   - a Marathon
   - b Torch
   - c Games

10. "Please slow ______ because you're driving too fast!"
    - a up
    - b down
    - c away

Exercise IV

In each question, combine the sentences using the correct conjunction from the options given without changing the order of the sentences. The answer is the option having the correct conjunction.

1. They got married. They had to learn to manage their own home.
   - a Therefore
   - b Earlier
   - c After
   - d For

2. Sandeep went crazy. His wife Meena burnt his breakfast.
   - a When
   - b Consequently
   - c Due
   - d Thus

3. You can hear what I'm saying. You keep quiet.
   - a But
   - b If
   - c And
   - d Although

4. We're broke. We can't buy anything.
   - a Since
   - b Earlier
   - c Thus
   - d Yet

5. He failed. He won't give up his ideals.
   - a Even though
   - b Since
   - c So
   - d And

6. I won't invite my classmates to a party. I know them well.
   - a Until
   - b As though
   - c But
   - d And

7. He fell asleep. He was watching the film.
   - a Thus
   - b While
   - c As soon as
   - d Since

8. He arrived home. I had already cleaned the house.
   - a By the time
   - b Where
   - c For
   - d However

9. She's snobbish. People like her.
   - a And
   - b Yet
   - c Thus
   - d Since

10. The first quiz was easy. This one is extremely difficult.
    - a Whereas
    - b Because
    - c Therefore
    - d Since

14 *Reading Comprehension*

Comprehension involves a thorough understanding of the given passage consisting of one or more paragraphs. It forms a very good exercise for thorough and intelligent reading, judicious selection and correct expression. It is meant to test the intelligence of students and the way of expressing their thoughts independently in a short, simple and precise manner. This type of exercise eliminate memorising and paves the way for precise writing.

While reading a comprehension, an individual's ability to comprehend text is influenced by skill. One of that skill is drawing inference. Apart from that, vocabulary and knowledge are other factors of attempting comprehension effectively.

In Olympiad, the comprehension passages include Multiple Choice Questions. Students have to select the best possible answer from the given choices. Here exercise of 12 passages is given. Each passage is followed by five questions; out of which two questions are fact based, two vocabulary based and one question is inference based.

Unless students have not understood the text clearly, they cannot find a suitable answer to the given questions. Given below are some steps to attempt questions of the comprehension.

Steps to Answer the Questions

Step 1   **Read** the title of the passage very carefully, if given. Determine what clues it gives you about the passage.

Step 2   **Watch for keywords** like causes, results, effects, etc. Do not overlook signal words such as those suggesting controversy (e.g., versus, pros and cons), which indicate that the author is intending to present both sides of an argument.

Step 3   **Skim** once as rapidly as possible to determine the main idea before you look at the questions. Do not worry about words you do not know at this stage.

Step 4   **Underline the words** that you do not understand to facilitate a complete understanding of the passage. This will enable you to solve the vocabulary related questions quicker.

Step 5   **Look** through **the words** carefully You are advised to maintain the order in which the questions appear in the test paper. Read intensively the portion relevant to the answer.

Step 6   **Concentrate** on the vocabulary items and **puzzle out** the meanings of those words you do not know in the context.

Step 7   Read the **questions** carefully and then try to find an answer from the passages.

Practice Centre

Passage I

Read the passage carefully and select the correct option in the given questions:

The sugar maple is a hard maple tree. It can grow as tall as 100 feet and as wide as 4 feet. The sugar maple is commercially valued for its sap, which is used in the making of maple syrup. Two states of the USA, Vermont and New York, rank as major producers of maple syrup. In Canada, the state of Quebec's annual syrup production is almost 1 million litres annually. To make pure maple syrup, holes are made in the trunk of the tree at the end of the winter or in early spring. The water-like sap seeps through the holes and runs through a plastic spout that is put into the hole. Afterwards, the collected sap is transferred into tubes that are hooked up to a tank kept in the sugar house. Then the sap goes through the boiling process.

Boiling enhances the flavour as well as adding colour to the sap. Once the sugar content of the sap is about 65-66%, the sap is ready to be strained and marketed. The maple syrup found in the supermarkets, however, is usually not pure and has other additives. The colour of pure maple may range from golden honey to light brown. Between 35 and 50 litres of sap are needed to produce 1 litre of maple syrup. Also popular for strength and finish of its wood, the sugar maple tree has been put to use in the making of furniture, interior woodwork, flooring and crates.

Questions

1. For which of the following words does the author provide a definition?
   - a The sugar maple
   - b A tank
   - c Additives
   - d Furniture

2. According to the passage, which of the following periods is ideal for sapping?
   - a Early November to late December
   - b February to early April
   - c May to late July
   - d August to early October

3. What can be inferred about the production of maple syrup?
   - a The higher the volume, the less predictable the quality
   - b It is labour intensive
   - c Its processing demands complicated equipment
   - d It is rather simple, but time-consuming

4. The word 'its' in the last sentence of the passage refers to
   - a sap
   - b maple syrup
   - c colour
   - d the sugar maple tree

5. Which of the following would best describe the organisation of the passage?
   - a A persuasive argument in favour of the maple syrup industry is advanced.
   - b A comparison and contrast between pure and commercial maple syrup is made.
   - c A step-by-step explanation of how maple syrup is made is given.
   - d A cause and effect analysis of the maple syrup production is presented.

Passage II

Read the passage carefully and select the correct option in the given questions:

The Alaska pipeline starts at the frozen edge of the Arctic Ocean. It stretches Southward across the largest and Northernmost state in the United States, ending at a remote ice-free seaport village nearly 800 miles from where it begins. It is massive in size and extremely complicated to operate.

The steel pipe crosses windswept plains and endless miles of delicate tundra that tops the frozen ground. It weaves through crooked canyons, climbs sheer mountains, plunges over rocky crags, makes its way through thick forests and passes over or under hundreds of rivers and streams. The pipe is 4 feet in diameter, and up to 2 million barrels (or 84 million gallons) of crude oil can be pumped through it daily.

ENGLISH **OLYMPIAD** CLASS VIII

Resting on H-shaped steel racks called 'bents', long sections of the pipeline follow a zigzag course high above the frozen earth. Other long sections drop out of sight beneath spongy or rocky ground and return to the surface later on. The pattern of the pipeline's up-and-down route is determined by the often harsh demands of the arctic and subarctic climate, the tortuous lay of the land, and the varied compositions of soil, rock, or permafrost (permanently frozen ground). A little more than half of the pipeline is elevated above the ground.

The remainder is buried anywhere from 3 to 12 feet, depending largely upon the type of terrain and the properties of the soil.

One of the largest in the world, the pipeline costs approximately $ 8 billion and is by far the biggest and most expensive construction project ever undertaken by private industry. In fact, no single business could raise that much money, so eight major oil companies formed a consortium in order to share the costs. Each company controlled oil rights to particular shares of land in the oil fields and paid into the pipeline construction fund according to the size of its holdings. Today, despite enormous problems of climate, supply shortages, equipment breakdowns, labour disagreements, treacherous terrain, a certain amount of mismanagement and even theft, the Alaska pipeline has been completed and is operating.

Questions

1. The meaning of the phrase 'drop out of sight' in the third paragraph is
   a go into exile
   b disappear from public view
   c fall below something and be no longer visible
   d go into hiding

2. The phrase 'resting on' in third paragraph is closest in meaning to
   a consisting of
   b supported by
   c passing under
   d protected with

3. Which one of the following determined what percentage of the construction costs each member of the consortium would pay?
   a How many oil wells were located on the company's land
   b How many people worked for each company
   c How long each company had owned land in the oil fields
   d How much oilfield land each company owned

4. Where in the passage does the author provide a term for an earth covering that always remains frozen?
   a Paragraph 1, sentence 2
   b Paragraph 3, sentence 1
   c Paragraph 3, sentence 3
   d Paragraph 4, last sentence

5. The passage primarily discusses the pipeline's
   a operating costs
   b employees
   c consumers
   d construction

Passage III

Read the comprehension based on a poem and select the correct option in the given questions:

Ring out, wild bells, to the wild sky,
The flying cloud, the frosty light:
The year is dying in the night;
Ring out, wild bells, and let him die.

Ring out the old, ring in the new,
Ring, happy bells, across the snow:
The year is going, let him go;
Ring out the false, ring in the true.

Ring out the grief that saps the mind,
For those that here we see no more;
Ring out the feud of rich and poor,
Ring in redress to all mankind.

Ring out a slowly dying cause,
And ancient forms of party strife;
Ring in the nobler modes of life,
With sweeter manners, purer laws.

–by Alfred, Lord Tennyson

Questions

1. What holiday would you associate with these lines?
   - a Easter holidays
   - b Summer holidays
   - c Christmas and New Year holidays
   - d None of the above

2. What kind of changes does Tennyson hope to see in the future?
   - a Changes which cause wars and bitterness
   - b Changes which cause people to become law-abiding
   - c Changes which make the rich fight with the poor
   - d Changes which cause happiness in all spheres of life

3. Which of the following does the poet not want to ring out?
   - a Good manners
   - b Quarrels between the poor and the rich
   - c Falsehood
   - d Sadness

4. What does 'redress' mean in this poem?
   - a Get dressed again / change clothes
   - b Clothing worn by an older person
   - c Making up for a wrong or injustice
   - d Playing melodious music

5. What is a feud, as given in the poem?
   - a An ongoing quarrel with bad feelings on each side
   - b A game that creates feelings of comfort
   - c A waterway that is similar to a deep river
   - d A home with separate living quarters for servants

Passage IV

Read the passage carefully and select the correct option in the given questions:

The consequence of a combination of overeating and physical inactivity is obesity. The extent to which obesity can adversely affect the health and well-being of a person is best exemplified by the modern day Nauruans, a small nation of 7000 once happy and healthy people of the tiny 20 square kilometre island country of Nauru in the Western Pacific.

Their small island was an equatorial paradise with lush green forests and waters full of fish. It had enough for everyone. Unfortunately, they suddenly found themselves rich beyond belief. Huge deposits of high-grade phosphate had been sighted in the island in the nineteenth century. In the past three decades, since independence, they have recklessly mined their country for phosphate for export and converted their beautiful country into a barren uninhabitable land.

With the money pouring in millions of dollars, they imported an incredible number of cars, gadgets and junk foods for easy and luxurious living, as well as brought labour to work for them. With plenty to eat and no work to do, the nation's active healthy people have converted themselves into sick and lethargic, fat and flabby men and women, many of whom weigh over 135 kilograms.

It is frightening but true that 50 per cent of the population has become diabetic and there is rampant hypertension and heart disease, cutting short their lifespan to an average of only 55 years. Now with the phosphate deposits having all but disappeared, their country converted into a barren wasteland and money no longer pouring in, it is not difficult to imagine their fate.

Though less glaring, the story of neo-affluent in other countries, including India, is not very different. Quick prosperity with physical inertia is a risky proposition.

Questions

1. Which activity has converted the island nation of Nauru into a barren wasteland?
   - a Import of cars, gadgets and junk food
   - b Plenty of eating and no work to do
   - c Living in an equatorial paradise
   - d Phosphate mining

2. The idiom 'rich beyond belief' in the second paragraph means
   - a not at all rich
   - b doubtful whether they are rich
   - c rich more than what is considered believable
   - d more affluent than before

  ENGLISH **OLYMPIAD** CLASS VIII

3. When the author says, "it is not difficult to imagine their fate" at the end of the fourth paragraph, what does he mean?

    a He means that their future is bleak

    b He means that their future is bright

    c He means that it is easy to understand how they became obese

    d He means that we can easily imagine that they are prosperous

4. Why does the author use the word, 'unfortunately' in the third sentence of the second paragraph?

    a It signifies that the Nauruans were unfortunate in having lush green forests and waters full of fish.

    b The author wants to say that the country was too small and thus unfortunate.

    c The author wants to say that the unbelievable wealth brought with it many bad consequences for the local population's health and the country's future.

    d The author wants to say that wealthy people are unfortunate.

5. Which of the following is an antonym of 'recklessly' used in the third paragraph?

    a Irresponsibly

    b Carefully

    c Daredevil

    d Extravagantly

Passage V

Read the passage carefully and select the correct option in the questions:

An Indian farmer is known as the second God because he produces different kinds of foodstuffs for us. No doubt, the financial condition of the big farmers has become better than a few years ago. However, an Indian farmer who has only a small holding is a poor, abject creature. The small farmers are often under heavy debt which they are unable to pay back. Being illiterate, a marginal farmer is normally unable to handle the situation through which he is passing. He keeps incurring loans all his life either to get his daughter married or to get his addicted son educated, and soon many such farmers themselves fall victims to bad habits like drinking and drug-taking. In this way, they go on becoming poorer and poorer. Some of them have to commit suicide, being unable to pay their debts.

The government is trying its best to save them from this devastating situation by providing them free water and electricity and also by giving them loans at low interest rates. But according to the government, the small farmers are unable to make hay while the sun shines because they have no tubewells of their own to avail themselves of these opportunities. So they have to buy water from the big farmers. Thus, one of the important sections of our country has been forced by circumstances to wallow in abject poverty.

Questions

1. What is the meaning of the idiom, "make hay while the sun shines" used in the second paragraph?

    a Produce hay to provide fodder to their animals

    b Use the tubewells which they have for irrigating their crops

    c Ripen their crops due to the sunshine

    d Make good use of opportunities while they last

2. For what reasons does a small farmer take loans?

    a For his drugs and drinks

    b For the marriage of his daughter

    c For repaying his debts

    d All of the above

3. Which of the following is / are reasons for a small farmer remaining poor?

    a He is an abject creature.

    b He is always under debts which he is unable to pay back.

    c He has to buy water from the big farmers.

    d Government provides him free water and electricity.

4. What is the effect of illiteracy on the small farmer?

    a He cannot manage the many crises he faces.

    b He is unable to grow a bountiful crop.

    c He cannot negotiate with the big. farmers regarding the price of water he buys from them.

    d All of the above

5. Which of the following is an antonym of 'abject' used in the third sentence of the first paragraph?

    a Miserable   b Pitiable

    c Proud   d Rich

Passage VI

Read the comprehension based on a poem and select the correct option in the given questions:

Did I Ever Stop?

Did I ever stop to make you smile
When your day was hard or your road was long?
When your light stopped shining for a while,
Did I sing for you a happy song?

Did I ever try to make you laugh
When your eyes held tears and you couldn't speak?
When your world seemed almost torn in half,
Did I hold your hand or kiss your cheek?

Did I ever pause to hear your voice
When you needed just a moment's ear?
When you'd lost your way or missed a choice,
Did I let you know that I was near?

Did I ever stop to say I care
When I didn't seek to hear it too?
When you weren't so sure that I'd be there,
Did I ever show my love for you?

Questions

1. The poet seems to be addressing someone who ____________.
- a likes to play
- b is happy
- c is feeling low
- d likes to sing

2. The poet sings ____________ song.
- a a happy
- b an unhappy
- c a sad
- d a melancholy

3. The poem is about ____________.
- a unimportant things like laughter
- b making others unhappy
- c being compassionate to others
- d one's own selfish interests

4. Which word in the poem means the same as 'ripped apart'?
- a Stop
- b Pull
- c Broken
- d Torn

5. The poet wants to know if he ever showed his ____________ for you.
- a infatuation
- b affection
- c hatred
- d benevolence

Passage VII

Read the passage carefully and select the correct option in the given questions:

The Time Travel Agency was the third room along the corridor. Simon Falk finally reached the pink glass doors. A notice outside read:

Simon stared into the interior and then went, reluctantly it seemed, inside. An assistant slid silently to his side the moment he was in the room, with hands clasped before him in deference to his customer.

"Can I help you, Sir?"

"Just some brochures, please. Can I take some away with me to, er, study at leisure?"

OUR PACKAGE TOURS OFFER YOU THE REMARKABLE!
THIS IS YOUR CHANCE TO SEE HISTORICAL EVENTS SUCH AS
- *The Battle of Marathon*
- *The Wars of the Roses*
- *The First Manned Space Flight*

ABSOLUTELY NO PERSONAL RISK!

"Certainly, sir." The fingers unravelled themselves and began deftly plucking multi-coloured sheets of paper from the display shelves with the expertise of a seasoned fruit-picker. "When you've made your mind up, perhaps you will give us a call and we will see what can be arranged. There is no need to come personally for the booking......" Simon wriggled uncomfortably. "I was just on my way home - I know I could have ordered them by mail, but my wife is impatient."

"Yes", the salesman smiled silkily. "Um, the Coronation of Elizabeth the First is fully booked, I'm afraid, and the Revolution of Mars has only a limited number of seats available."

"I don't believe we are interested in those events," said Simon.

"Your first time, sir?" "Yes, as a matter of fact it is."

"Then may I recommend the Sacking of Carthage? We mingle with the camp followers on a neighbouring slope. However, I must add that it's not for the squeamish."

Simon asked, "Isn't that a little dangerous?"

"Er, no, not as long as you follow our little instructions." The agent wagged a finger playfully. "We've never lost a customer yet."

Questions

1. Which of the following best describes Simon's manner when he visited the Time Travel Agency?

   a Despondent   b Captivated

   c Awkward   d Respectful

2. Simon visited the Agency personally because

   a he wanted to get some brochures for his wife quickly.

   b he wanted to discuss package tours for his wife and himself.

   c he wanted to book seats while they were still available.

   d he was curious about what was behind the pink doors.

3. The word 'squeamish' used near the end of the passage means

   a absent-minded

   b easily upset by unpleasant sights

   c highly forgetful

   d extremely cautious

4. In what manner did the salesman at the Time Travel Agency perform his duties?

   a Haphazardly   b Laboriously

   c Indifferently   d Confidently

5. The word 'deference' used in the second paragraph means the same as

   a ignorance   b respectful

   c open refusal   d variance

Passage VIII

Read the passage carefully and select the correct option in the given questions:

We were finally within a day's drive of our destination. The truck climbed narrow winding roads into the mountains, above the patchwork of intense cultivation on the small farms below.

We plunged into Bwindi National Park. The trees spread their towering branches over the track, casting a dark gloom below. We drove on, surprised by the apparent lack of visible wildlife that we had grown used to in Africa. We glimpsed only the white flash of two monkey tails disappearing into the shadows. The quiet, when we stopped to camp for the night, was deafening.

The next day was visiting day. We set off on foot to a nearby village to start our trek. We had no idea, and neither did our local guides, how far we would have to hike. We meandered up the steep mountain on a constricted track made slippery by the recent rain. One misstep and you could slide on the mud all the way to the bottom of the valley, unless a banana tree halted your downward progress! But we were galvanised by one purpose: to see a family of Mountain Gorillas in the wild.

At the top of the mountain, we turned our backs on civilisation and entered the forest. After an hour of pushing through thick grass and spiny bushes, we happened upon our first gorillas. We were taken by surprise. Three young individuals looked at us curiously, with no sense of alarm. After examining us with penetrating stares, they turned and leapt into the undergrowth.

Our next encounter was with two youngsters wrestling each other. Engrossed in their play, they took not the slightest notice as we surrounded them, with cameras clicking in overdrive.

At last, in a more open part of the forest, we stumbled across the rest of the clan: the old man silverback, a number of females and youngsters of various ages.

A silverback is the strong, dominant leader of his family troop which typically comprises 5 to 30 individuals. As leader, he makes all the decisions and mediates in any conflicts. He controls the movements of the group and leads them to feeding sites, generally taking responsibility for their safety.

We sat and watched him and his family with reverence, aware of the great privilege he was allowing us; he just sat and watched us.

Questions

1. Where did the truck take the author's group?
   - a To the top of the mountain
   - b To the gorillas' home
   - c To the camp site
   - d To the village

2. What surprised the author during the truck journey?
   - a The gorillas avoided contact with people
   - b There seemed to be very few animals in the National Park
   - c The monkeys on the trees were unfamiliar to the author's group
   - d The branches hid all the animals in the shadows

3. What is the effect of the exclamation mark at the end of the fifth sentence in the third paragraph?
   - a It indicates the slim chances of the event ever occurring
   - b It highlights the author's fear of heights
   - c It suggests the writer's sense of disbelief
   - d It emphasises the humour of a potentially risky situation

4. Which of the following options has two words from the text which are similar in meaning?
   - a 'Plunged' and 'meandered'
   - b 'Surprise' and 'alarm'
   - c 'Constricted' and 'narrow'
   - d 'Engrossed' and 'galvanised'

5. When the author describes the quietness of the jungle as 'deafening' (end of second paragraph), he means that it was
   - a noticeable
   - b menacing
   - c mysterious
   - d permanent

Passage IX

Read the passage carefully and select the correct option in the given questions:

One of the main reasons of corruption in elections today is the lure of power which haunts the politicians so much that they feel no qualms of conscience in adopting any underhand method to come out successful. The Watergate scandal in the USA is an eloquent example to testify to the fact of how even the top level politicians can stoop to the lowest level in order to maintain themselves in power. Who does not remember how Adolf Hitler rode roughshod over all canons of electoral propriety to capture power?

In India also, the record of the various political parties is not clean. Corruption thrives in elections because those in the field play on the psychology of the electorate. The voters are swayed by the tall promises of the candidates to whose machinations they fall an easy prey. They are also susceptible to fall an easy prey to the adulations of the politicians due to their illiteracy. Besides, in representative democracies today, and particularly in large countries, the constituencies are quite extensive, obviating the possibility of corrupt practices being discovered. Anti-corruption laws are honoured more in their breach than in their observance. Even the code of conduct to be observed by the parties fighting the elections becomes a dead letter in as much as it is jettisoned out of existence and thrown unscrupulously overboard by the unfair politicians, whose only aim is to maintain themselves in the saddle.

Questions

1. Politicians indulge in corruption in elections now-a-days because
   - a elections can only be won by corrupt means
   - b of lure of power
   - c of lure of money
   - d corrupt practices in elections go unnoticed

2. How did Adolf Hitler come to power?
   - a By organising a mass movement
   - b By liquidating the opposition
   - c By using foreign help
   - d As a result of bungling in elections

3. How does corruption thrive in elections?
   - a Because the people themselves are corrupt
   - b Because there is a natural connection between elections and corruption
   - c By the politicians exploiting the electorate psychologically
   - d By the politicians cheating the electorate economically

4. The phrase, "to maintain themselves in the saddle"
    in the last sentence of the passage means
    a to retain power in their hands by continuing in
       office
    b to play an unfair game
    c to oust the opposition at every cost
    d to be ready to run whenever danger is apprehended

5. Which of the following is a synonym of
    'honoured' used in the second
    paragraph?
    a Commended
    b Criticised
    c Applauded
    d Obeyed

Passage X

Read the passage carefully and select the correct option in the given questions:

True, it is the function of the army to maintain law and order in abnormal times. But in normal times, there is another force that compels citizens to obey the laws and to act with due regard to the rights of others. This force also protects the lives and the properties of law-abiding men.

Laws are made to secure the personal safety of a country's citizens and to prevent murders or other crimes of violence. They are made to secure the property of the citizens against theft and damage, as well as to protect the rights of communities and castes to carry out their customs and ceremonies so long as they do not conflict with the rights of others. The good citizen, of his own free will, will obey these laws and take care that everything he does is done with due regard to the rights and well-being of others. But the bad citizen is only restrained from breaking these laws by the fear of the consequence of his actions. The necessary steps to compel the bad citizen to act as a good citizen are taken by this force. The supreme control of law and order in a state is in the hands of a minister who is responsible to the State Assembly and acts through the Inspector General of Police.

Questions

1. According to the writer, which one of the following
    is not the responsibility of the police?
    a To protect the privileges of all citizens
    b To check violent activities of citizens
    c To ensure peace among citizens by safeguarding
       individual rights
    d To maintain peace during extraordinary
       circumstances

2. Which of the following statements expresses most
    accurately the idea contained in the first sentence?
    a It is the job of the army to ensure internal peace at
       all times.
    b It is the police that should always enforce law and
       order in the country.
    c It is in exceptional circumstances that the army
       has to ensure peace in the country.
    d Army and the police ensure people's security
       through combined operations.

3. Which of the following is not mentioned or
    implied in the passage?
    a The forces of law help to transform irresponsible
       citizens into responsible ones.
    b A criminal is deterred from committing crimes only
       due to fear of the law.

    c The law protects those who respect it.
    d The law ensures people's religious and
       social rights absolutely and
       unconditionally.

4. Which of the following options has the
    opposite meaning to the word
    'restrained' in the second paragraph?
    a Inhibited   b Accelerated
    c Promoted   d Intruded

5. In the second sentence of the second
    paragraph, the phrase, "they are made
    to secure the property of citizens
    against theft and damage" means that
    the laws
    a safeguard people's possessions against
       being stolen or damaged.
    b help in recovering the stolen property
       of the citizens
    c initiate the process against offenders
       of law.
    d assist the citizens whose property has
       been stolen or destroyed.

<h1 align="center">Passage XI</h1>

Read the passage carefully and select the correct option in the given questions:

The profession of pharmacy was founded in the art and science of compounding medications. The beginning of compounding dates back to medieval times with priests, monks, and medicine men, with specialisation first occurring in the early ninth century in the civilised world around Baghdad. During this time, doctors began prescribing medications to patients. Pharmacists then began compounding these prescriptions and producing them in mass quantities for general sale. However, it was not until the 19th century that there was a distinct difference between the pharmacist as a compounder of medications and the physician as the therapist. In the 1930s and 1940s, approximately 60 percent of all medications dispensed were compounded. Then in the 1950s and 1960s, with the creation of commercial drug manufacturers, compounding declined. It was during this time that a pharmacist, known as a compounder or apothecary, became known as a dispenser of manufactured drugs. However, today patients and doctors are realising the need for specific doses and customised medications, and because of this, pharmacists are once again gaining the reputation once bestowed upon them prior to the commercialisation of generic compound drugs in the 1950s.

Questions

1. Which of the following is the idea conveyed by the passage as a whole?
   a A pharmacist is a compounder of medicines
   b Iraq is the birthplace of modern pharmacology
   c Pharmacy is an ancient occupation
   d Pharmacists' perceived roles have wavered over the last few centuries

2. Which of the following is neither stated nor implied in the passage?
   a Specific doses are best handled on a case-by-case basis
   b Commercial drug manufacturers first became abundant in the 1950s & 1960s
   c Compounding dates back to ancient times
   d Compounding is the science of combining medicines

3. When was a distinct difference observed between the roles of a physician and a pharmacist?
   a During the 19th centur
   b During the early ninth century
   c In the 1950s and 1960s
   d In the 1930s and 1940s

4. According to the passage, which of the following is the intended meaning of the word 'therapist' in the last sentence of the first paragraph?
   a A person having knowledge about the proper ratio in which two medicines should be combined
   b A medical doctor who can diagnose an illness but who has limited knowledge on the specific medicine that should be prescribed
   c A trusted individual who makes informed medicinal decisions
   d A layman who diagnoses illnesses and prescribes medications

5. Which of the following is a synonym of 'bestowed' used in the last sentence of the passage?
   a Donated   b Accorded
   c Removed   d Desired

Passage XII

Read the comprehension based on a poem carefully and select the correct option in the given questions:

The sun descending in the west,
The evening star does shine;
The birds are silent in their nest.
And I must seek for mine.

The moon, like a flower
In heaven's high bower,
With silent delight
Sits and smiles on the night.

Farewell, green fields and happy grove,
Where flocks have took delight:
Where lambs have nibbled, silent move
The feet of angels bright;

Unseen they pour blessing
And joy without ceasing
On each bud and blossom,
And each sleeping bosom.

They look in every thoughtless nest
Where birds are covered warm;
They visit caves of every beast,
To keep them all from harm:

If they see any weeping
That should have been sleeping,
They pour sleep on their head,
And sit down by their bed. —*by William Blake*

Questions

1. The evening star rises when __________.
    - a the birds leave their nests
    - b it is midnight
    - c the sun descends in the west
    - d it is dawn

2. The birds' nest is described as 'thoughtless' because __________.
    - a the occupants are asleep without any care
    - b the birds are covered in the warmth of their nest
    - c the nest has been made without any thought
    - d the angels are blessing the birds

3. The angels come down on earth to __________.
    - a spread the moonlight
    - b give blessings and joy
    - c make people dance and have fun
    - d take the blessings of the people

4. The figure of speech used in the line 'In heaven's high bower' is __________.
    - a personification
    - b alliteration
    - c simile
    - d metaphor

5. In the second stanza the 'bower' represents __________.
    - a a bouquet of flowers
    - b a flower vase
    - c a potted plant
    - d a framework supporting climbing plants

15

Writing Skills

Here the following formats of composition are covered which are asked in examinations:

    I. Letters   II. E-Mail   III. Notice

Letters

Letters are broadly classified into **informal** and **formal** letters.

Informal letters include personal letters to

- Relatives
- Colleagues
- Friends and acquaintances

Formal letters include

- Business letters - enquiries asking for quotations, their replies, placing orders, etc.
- Official letters - conveying information to people holding office
- Applications for jobs
- Letters to editors of newspapers / magazines
- Complaints to authorities for redress

The format of a formal letter is given below as an example.

B-12, Indraprastha Apartments 21, Paschim Vihar New Delhi-110063	**Letter writer's address** *Sender's address is written here. Never put your name here*
20th March, 20XX	**Date** *The date appears directly below the address after leaving a line*
The Editor The Indian Express New Delhi	**Receiver's name/rank and his/her address**
Subject *Female Foeticide : Undoing of Humanity*	**Subject of the letter** *Indicate the Theme/Subject here*
Sir/Madam	**Salutation** *It is a customary greeting with which the sender opens the letter*
Through the columns of your esteemed newspaper, I wish to share my concern about the killing of the girl foetus before birth. *Undoubtedly, in the post-independence era, Indian woman has altered her image of being vulnerable and illiterate. Still the male chauvinism, which is rampant in our society is indulging in female foeticide, leading to alarming decrease in the female population.* *Recent surveys have clearly shown that sex determination tests are widely practised. They slaughter the girl before she is born, just because they want a son. In states like Haryana and Rajasthan, the situation is really dismal where brides are being 'bought' from other states for marriages leading to human trafficking.*	**Body of the letter** *Always change the para while making a new point.*
It's time to take stringent measures to check this vehement killing of the girl foetus. I hope that my thoughts find some space in the reader's column.	**Conclusion** *Having hope/comment request*
Yours sincerely **Kusum**	**Subscription and Signature** *Name and designation, if applicable*

The format of an informal letter is given below as an example.

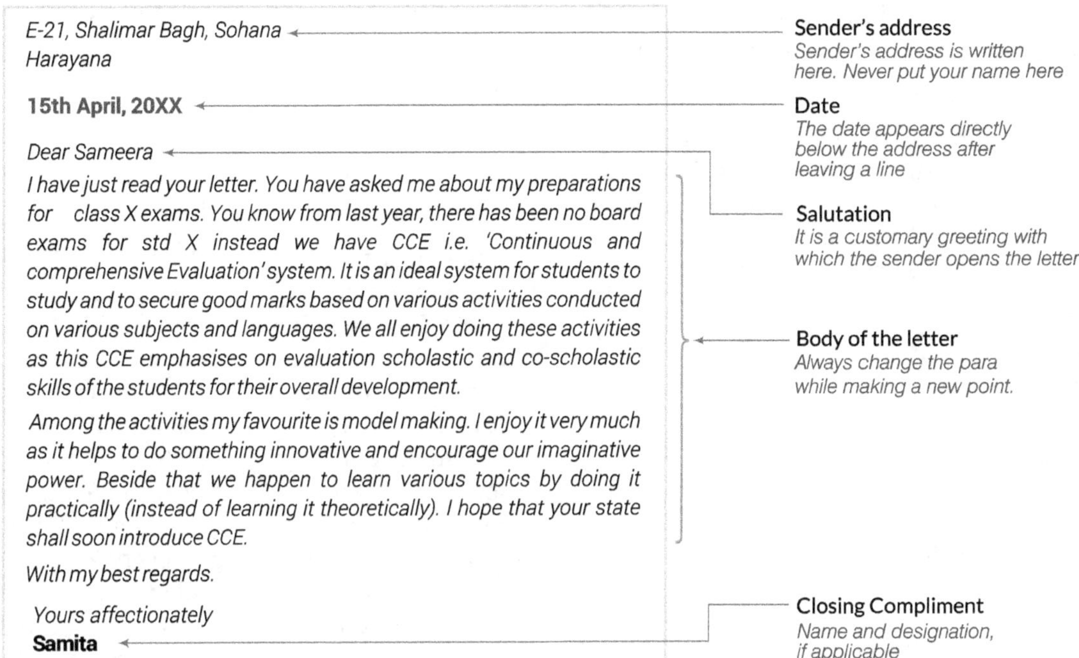

Practice Centre

Exercise I Letters

A. *The parts of a formal letter are identified by numbers in the blank official letter format given below. Answer the questions 1 to 5 given below by selecting the correct option.*

1. The item identified as '2' is
   a sender's address   **b** subscription
   c salutation   **d** date

2. The item identified as '1' is
   a receiver's name   **b** receiver's address
   c body of letter   **d** theme of letter

3. The item identified as '3' is
   a sender's address   **b** signature
   c salutation   **d** date

4. The item identified as '7' is
   a sender's name   **b** body of letter
   c subject of letter   **d** subscription

5. The item identified as '6' is
   a receiver's name/rank
   b receiver's address
   c salutation
   d theme of letter

B. *A letter is given here with six blanks 1, 2, 3, 4, 5, 6 which should be filled by statements A, B, C, D, E, F. Choose your answer from the given options.*

A letter to the Editor, The Times of India, Delhi expresses your concern over the increase in the rate of road accidents, rash driving and suggest ways to curb accidents. You are Nandita/Naveen of 15, Jawahar Nagar, New Delhi.

15, Jawahar Nagar
New Delhi
5th December, 2015

The Editor
The Times of India
New Delhi

Subject: ______1______

Sir,

Through the columns of your esteemed newspaper, I would like to express my views on ___2___ and overcrowded transport in the city.

Everyday, we hear of road accidents and deaths due to accidents. It is only due to the ___3___ of the drivers. Drinking and driving can't go together. But unfortunately drivers drive very rashly, often under the influence of liquor, ___4___. This is the major reason for road accidents. Most of the drivers ignore road cautions and signals. ___5___. They can't be left at the mercy of drunk drivers. The ___6___. The traffic police need to be streamlined and made an effective force. There is also a need for regular patrolling.

I think that the authorities will definitely look into this problem and try to check this problem.

Yours sincerely
Nandita

    (a) not at all caring for traffic rules
    (b) Increase in the rate of road accidents
    (c) Human lives are precious
    (d) erring drivers should be given exemplary punishment.
    (E) the increase in the rate of road accidents
    (F) carelessness and slackness

Choose your answer from the given options:

    a BCEAFD
    b BEFACD
    c CDAFEB
    d AFECDB

C. *In the following letter, the linking words and phrases are missing. Choose the most appropriate phrase to be filled in each blank from the options given.*

25, Banjara Road
Hyderabad 500034

Dear Rakesh,

Remember that I told you I was trying to get a job at Dell Computers. **1.**_____ I finally managed to get one! Of course, I haven't been working there long, **2.**_____ I can already tell that it's a wonderful place to work in. All the staff **3.**_____ directors are very friendly and **4.**_____, they have marvellous facilities for employees. **5.**_____ there's a bar and gym, and lots of other things. I'm called the Senior Safety Equipment Officer. It **6.**_____ sound like an impressive title, but it's not a very **7.**_____ of what I do. My main job is to provide protective clothing, **8.**_____ overalls, helmets and so on. I estimate what the different departments will need and **9.**_____ I order it from the **10.**_____.

11._____ I make sure that the various departments have everything they want. **12.**_____ I have to supply all the offices with paper, envelopes and so on. I find the job **13.**_____ because I get the chance to go all over the factory and meet everyone. **14.**_____ the pay is far better than in my old job. **15.**_____, that's my news. What about yours? Drop me a line when you have time.

Regards to your parents and best wishes to you.
Abhijit Narang

1.   a Then   b Well
     c And   d So

2.   a but   b because
     c and   d or

3.   a until   b till
     c and   d ever

4.   a what's more   b therefore
     c moreover   d so

5.   a For instance   b However
     c Moreover   d Ever

6.   a can   b could
     c may   d might

7.   a fine account   b accurate description
     c correct picture   d fine description

8.   a namely   b as
     c such as   d like

9.   a then   b so
     c so that   d after

<table>
<tr><td>

10.   a supply branch   b distribution
      c suppliers   d person

</td><td>

13.   a very boring   b interesting
      c dull   d mind boggling

</td></tr>
<tr><td>

11.   a By the way   b Any way
      c However   d In this way

</td><td>

14.   a Besides   b On the other hand
      c In contrast   d Beside

</td></tr>
<tr><td>

12.   a But   b Although
      c However   d Secondly

</td><td>

15.   a After all   b somehow
      c Anyway   d at the end

</td></tr>
</table>

D. *Choose the correct options to fill the given blanks in the letter given below.*

Fashion Quarterly Magazine, Sant Nagar
Mumbai 400001

1._____________

Ms Kavita **2.**_____________
741, MG Road
Mumbai 400079

      3.___________

Dear Ms Kapoor

Thank you for your letter **4.**______ 18th July, 20XX regarding non-receipt of the **5.**______. We have contacted our distribution agent regarding this problem and **6.**______. Meanwhile we are enclosing the missing issue of the magazine with this letter. We regret the **7.**______.

8.___________
Circulation manager

<table>
<tr><td>

1.   a 25th July, 20XX   b Maharashtra, July
     c 2017/2014

2.   a Menon   b Maheshwari
     c Kapoor

3.   a Untimely delivery of magazine
     b Non-delivery of magazine
     c Delivery of magazine

4.   a dated
     b written on
     c delivered

</td><td>

5.   a January issue of Fashion Quarterly Magazine
     b Many issues of Fashion Quarterly Magazine
     c July issue of Fashion Quarterly Magazine

6.   a will be back to you shortly
     b will convey to you shortly
     c will get back to you shortly

7.   a problems caused   b inconvenience caused
     c delay in the delivery

8.   a Yours dearly   b Yours obediently
     c Yours sincerely

</td></tr>
</table>

E-mail

E-mails are a popular way of communication nowadays, used for formal as well as informal communication. They can be conveyed much faster than conventional letters. Because e-mails use a computer or smartphone for sending and receiving communications, users need to follow certain computer related conventions.

A typical e-mail composing screen is shown below.

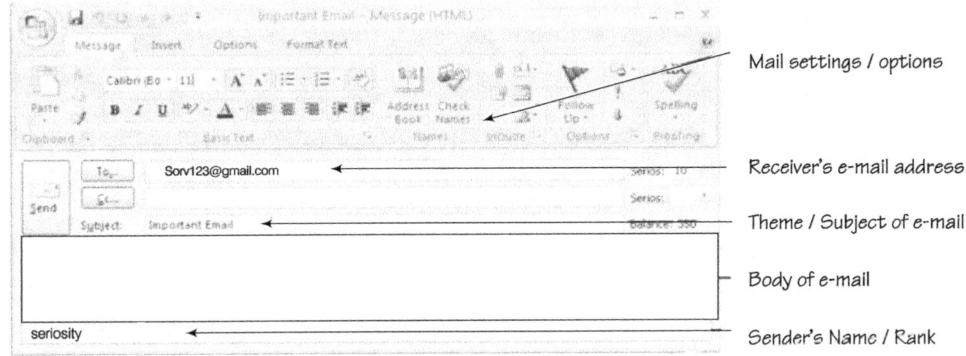

Exercise **II** E-mail

A. *An e-mail to be sent is given below with some parts missing, but substituted by numbers 1, 2, 3, 4 or 5. Identify the numbers by selecting the correct options from those given below.*

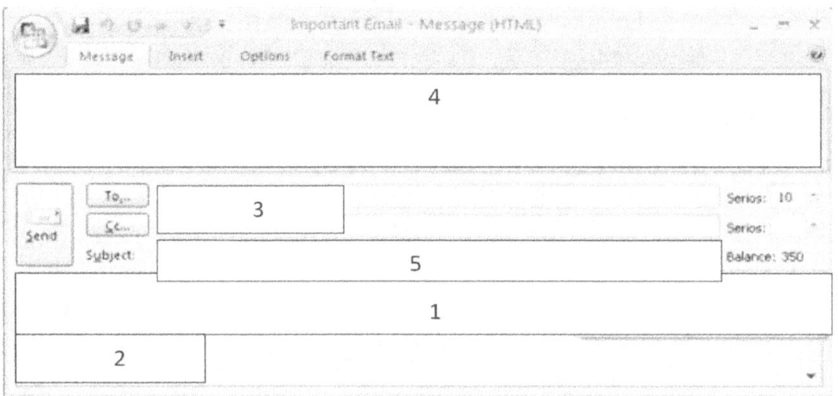

1. The item identified as '1' is
   a Mail settings / options   **b** Receiver's e-mail address
   c Theme / Subject of e-mail   **d** Body of e-mail

2. The item identified as '2' is
   a Sender's Name / Rank   **b** Receiver's e-mail address
   c Theme / Subject of e-mail   **d** Body of e-mail

3. The item identified as '3' is
   a Theme / Subject of e-mail   **b** Receiver's e-mail address
   c Mail settings / options   **d** Body of e-mail

4. The item identified as '4' is
   a Sender's Name / Rank   **b** Receiver's e-mail address
   c Mail settings / options   **d** Body of e-mail

5. The item identified as '5' is
   a Mail settings / options   **b** Receiver's e-mail address
   c Theme / Subject of e-mail   **d** Body of e-mail

B. *You are Amarjeet Singh, H.R. manager of a company. Send an e-mail to the employees of your company about the problem of too many personal calls being made by the employees. There are certain blanks which are to be filled in by you by selecting them from the given options.*

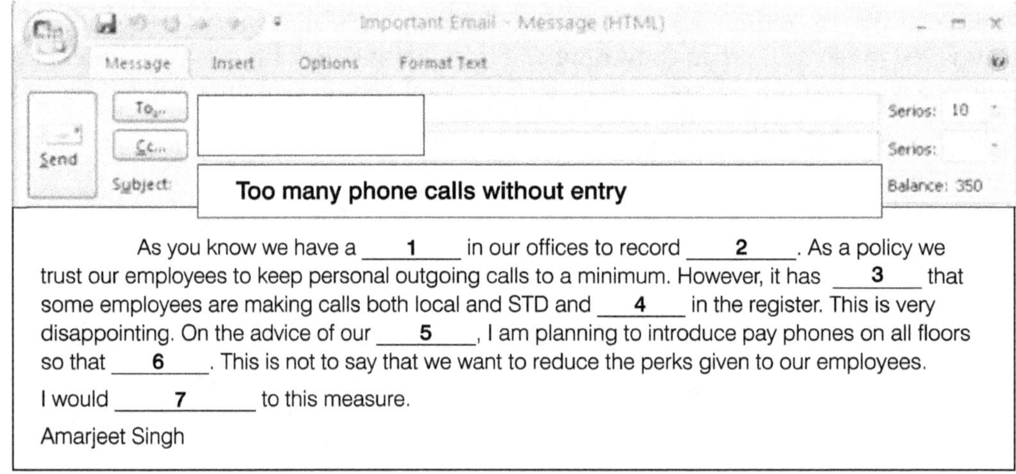

1.   **a**   attendance register   **b**   entry register   **c**   phone call register

2.   **a**   outgoing calls   **b**   incoming calls   **c**   all the calls

3.   **a**   came to my notice   **b**   has been brought to my notice
    c   come to my knowledge

4.   **a**   not entering calls   **b**   not making entry   **c**   not mentioning in the register

5.   **a**   HR department   **b**   Law department   **c**   Personnel department

6.   **a**   all phone calls are paid for   **b**   all phone calls are registered
    c   all phone calls are charged for

7.   **a**   appreciate a positive response from you   **b**   appreciate any objection from any one
    c   appreciate any other suggestion from any one of you

Notice

A notice is a form of written communication used to convey information about functions, events or occasions, or used to announce something that has happened or is about to happen. Notices are generally displayed in prominent places. *The format of a typical notice is shown below.*

Format of a Notice

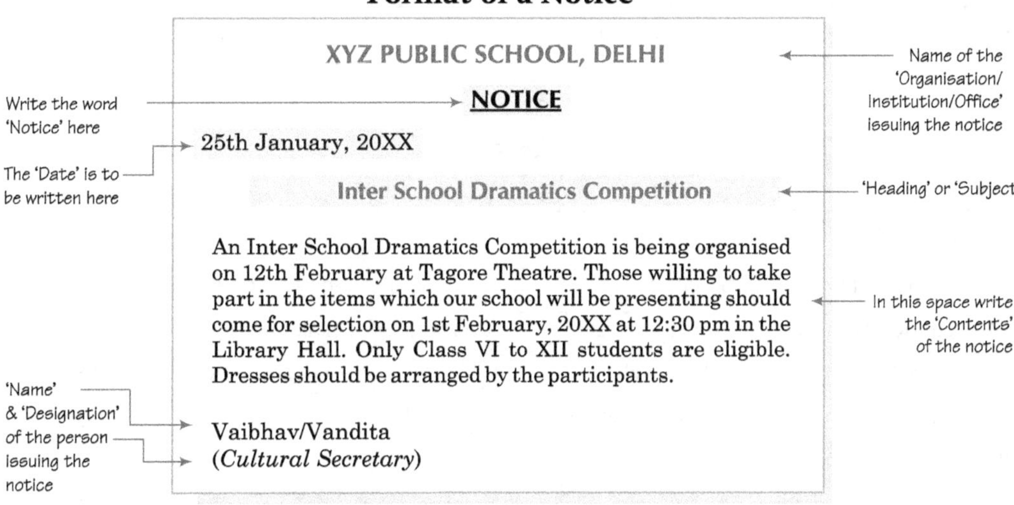

Exercise III   Notice

A. *A notice is given below with some parts missing, but substituted by numbers 1, 2, 3, 4 or 5. Identify the numbers by selecting the correct options from those given below.*

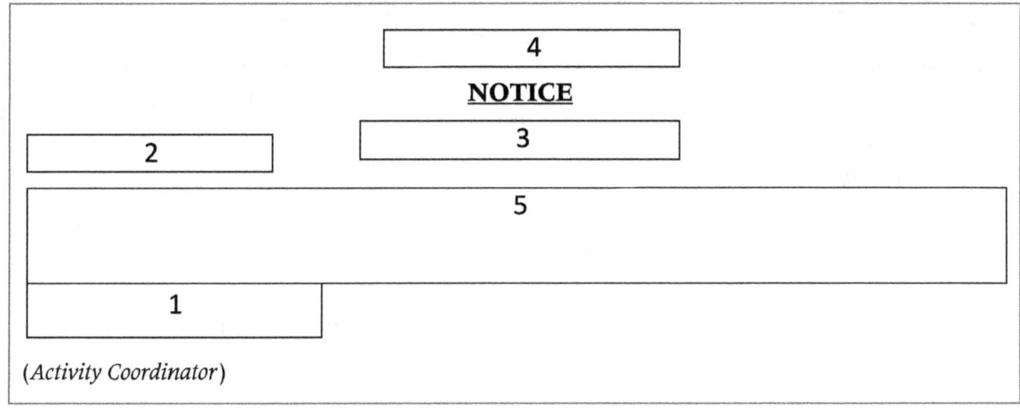

1. The item identified as '1' is
   a Name of the organisation
   b Name of issuer of the notice
   c Subject of the notice
   d Designation of issuer of the notice

2. The item identified as '2' is
   a Date of the notice
   b Subject of the notice
   c Contents of the notice
   d Designation of issuer of the notice

3. The item identified as '3' is
   a Name of the Organisation
   b Name of issuer of the notice
   c Subject of the notice
   d Date of the notice

4. The item identified as '4' is
   a Subject of the notice
   b Designation of issuer of the notice
   c Contents of the notice
   d Name of the organisation

5. The item identified as '5' is
   a Date of the notice
   b Name of issuer of the notice
   c Subject of the notice
   d Contents of the notice

B. *A notice on the subject 'Blood Donation' has been issued by the Red Cross Blood Bank Society, which is given below with some parts missing, but numbered 6 to 13. The options for these missing words / phrases are given below the notice. Select the correct options to fill in the missing parts.*

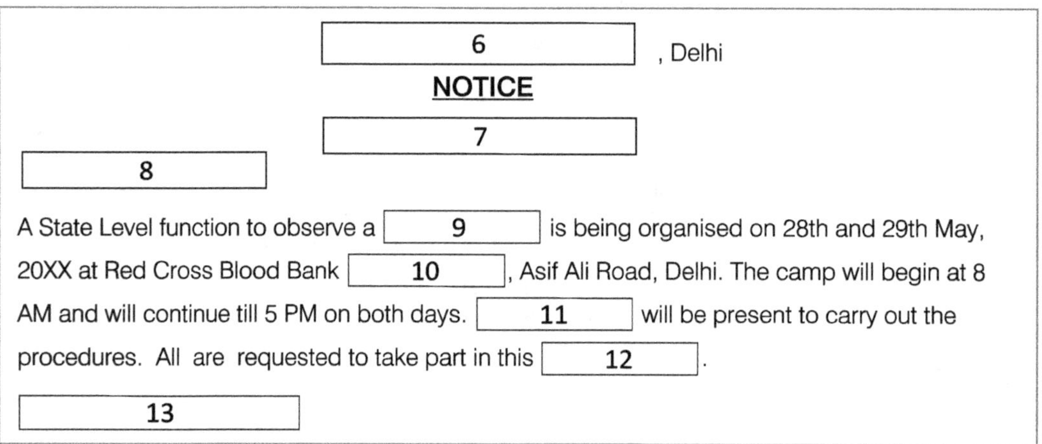

6. a Salutation
    b Name of governing body
    c Both (a) and (b)
    d Name of event

7. a Name of event
    b Name of governing body
    c Both (a) and (b)
    d Salutation

8. a 20th May, 20XX
    b January 2014
    c Dear Sir
    d This is to inform everyone

9. a compulsory blood donation day
    b voluntary blood donation day
    c partial blood donation day
    d government blood donation day

10. a Blood bank office
    b Society office
    c Blood bank hospital
    d Blood donation camp

11. a A team of specialised doctors
    b a team of doctors and assistants
    c a team of volunteer doctors
    d a team of doctors and people

12. a great cause
    b noble cause
    c greedy cause
    d money-making cause

13. a Donator
    b President
    c Social activist
    d Society officer

English **OLYMPIAD** CLASS VIII

C. You are the Sports Secretary of Laxman Public School, Noida. Your school is organising a regional level Volleyball Tournament for 4 days. Draft a notice in not more than 50 words inviting the students to come and cheer the teams and participants. The notice is given below with some parts missing which are numbered. *Choose the answer from the given options.*

1

NOTICE

6th December, 20XX

2

This is [3] all the students that a regional level Volleyball Tournament is being

[4] by the school from 9th December to 12th December, 20XX from 9 AM to 4

PM. All the students [5] to come and [6] by cheering for the

teams. For more information contact the [7] .

Anu Deshmukh

[8]

1. a Salutation   b Name of event
     c Both (a) and (b)   d Name of school

2. a Name of school   b Name of event
     c Salutation   d Both (b) and (c)

3. a to inform   b to aware
     c to know   d None of these

4. a organised   b designed
     c celebrated   d All of these

5. a are requested   b are ordered
     c are to report   d must come

6. a hoot the participants   b encourage the participants
     c discourage the participants   d shout for participants

7. a undersigned   b undermentioned
     c below signed   d signed

8. a Cultural Secretary   b Sportsman
     c Sports Secretary   d Sportswoman

Practice
Sets

Practice Set ①

A Whole Content Based Test for Class 8th English Olympiad

Directions for Q (1-5)   *Read the passage carefully and select the option that you consider the most appropriate answer to each question.*

The Story of Aspirin

Before people started using aspirin as a drug to relieve pain, there was willow bark. About 400 BC, Hippocrates, the 'father of medicine', advised chewing it to ease the pain of childbirth. For centuries, people all over the world knew of its power to treat headache, fever and inflammation. However, they did not understand why it had this power.

Through the 19th century, Chemistry became an important development in science. In Germany in the 1820s, the magic chemical in willow bark was isolated and named *salicin*. Later in the century, a drug, *acetylsalicyclic acid*, was developed, but no one really knew what to do with it. Some people tried a crude form of the drug which, they said, burned in their stomachs like acid.

Then a young chemist at the German chemical firm of Bayer & Company decided to try *acetylsalicyclic acid* on his father, who had arthritis. The wonder drug, aspirin, was born!

Why it was named *aspirin* is still debated. One theory is that the word came from *spiraea*, the plant from which *salicin* was actually isolated. The first aspirin tablets that people could buy from chemists' shops appeared at the beginning of the 20th century.

Questions

1. What does the first sentence of the passage tell us?
  - a People have always known about both willow bark and aspirin as pain relievers.
  - b People used willow bark to ease pain before aspirin was developed.
  - c Long ago, people knew how to use aspirin to relieve pain.
  - d Since ancient days people knew how to extract aspirin from willow bark.

2. In the second sentence of the passage, the word 'it' refers to ________.
  - a a drug
  - b medicine
  - c aspirin
  - d willow bark

3. According to the passage, Hippocrates knew ________.
  - a why willow bark could ease pain
  - b how willow bark could be processed
  - c what willow bark could be used for
  - d All of the above

4. The word 'wonder' used in the third paragraph is nearest in meaning to ________.
  - a marvellous
  - b admiration
  - c surprise
  - d sensation

5. According to the passage, "The wonder drug, aspirin, was born!" when a young German chemist ________.
  - a was able to produce *acetylsalicyclic acid*
  - b was able to prevent his father's arthritis
  - c used *acetylsalicyclic acid* to reduce his father's pain
  - d produced a drug combining *salicin* and *acetylsalicyclic acid*

6. *In the passage below, the first and last sentences are identified as A and Z. The remaining four sentences are labelled as P, Q, R and S. Find the correct sequence of these four sentences and select the correct option accordingly.*
  A The Hound of the Baskervilles was feared by people of the area.
  P The animal's shadowy silhouette did not reveal any details about it.
  Q Nobody had in reality seen the hound.
  R Some people spoke of seeing a huge, shadowy form of a hound at midnight on the moor.
  S And they spoke of it in tones of grave horror.
  Z Thus the hound remained a perplexing mystery.
  - a PQRS
  - b QPSR
  - c RPQS
  - d RSQP

7. *Find the option which is different from the others in any respect in the four given options. This means that one of the four given options does not belong to the group of the other three.*
  - a Duckling
  - b Chicken
  - c Goat
  - d Calf

Directions for Q (8-9) *Select the option having the meaning nearest to the idioms underlined in the given sentences.*

8. The celebratory party got <u>out of hand</u>, so we had to abruptly end it.
   a out of control
   b short of food
   c short of hands
   d restrained

9. Karan was <u>in hot water</u>, as he forgot to finish his homework.
   a clean
   b bathed properly
   c happy
   d in trouble

10. *Change the sentence given below into reported speech and accordingly select the best option.*

   "I slipped and fell down the stairs yesterday", said Sharmila.
   a Sharmila remarked that she had slipped and fallen down the stairs yesterday.
   b Sharmila said that she has slipped and fallen down the stairs yesterday.
   c Sharmila said that she had slipped and fallen down the stairs the previous day.
   d Sharmila was saying that she slipped and fell down the stairs the previous day.

11. *Change the sentence given below into a simple sentence and accordingly select the best option.*

   It was raining heavily, so many trains were cancelled.
   a It was raining heavily due to which many trains were cancelled.
   b On account of heavy rains, many trains were cancelled.
   c Accounting for the heavy rains, many trains were cancelled.
   d Many trains were cancelled due to the heavy rain.

12. *Change the sentence given below to passive voice using the underlined verb as subject and accordingly select the best option.*

   They still deny <u>women</u> the right to vote in Switzerland.
   a Switzerland does not allow women to have voting rights.
   b Switzerland does not allow women to have the right to vote.
   c Women in Switzerland can't vote.
   d Women are still denied the right to vote in Switzerland.

Directions for Q (13-14) *Find the synonyms for the words underlined in the sentences below and accordingly select the best option.*

13. The <u>benevolent</u> industrialist offered many scholarships for bright school students to study medicine.
   a generous   b industrious
   c helpful   d kind

14. The homes of the Bedouins are <u>portable</u> because the tribe is nomadic.
   a temporary   b tough
   c transportable d convenient

Directions for Q (15-16) *Identify the grammatically incorrect sentence from the given options.*

15. a The constructed new bridge took three years.
    b Animals make the most complicated homes.
    c The result of the first experiment was satisfactory.
    d Eradication of poverty is the need of the hour.

16. a His rudeness reinforced my determination to leave him.
    b She was in complete bewilderment when her husband suddenly left her.
    c This drug has absolutely no chemical similarity to any other drug.
    d Names of players who will be included in team have been announced.

Directions for Q (17-18) *Fill in the blanks with the most appropriate modal and accordingly select the best option.*

17. You ________ to be punctual.
    a should   b ought c would   d must

18. He _____ play cricket in his youth.
    a used to   b was used to
    c is used to   d were used to

Directions for Q (19-20) *Fill in the blanks with the most appropriate article (a / an / the / no article required) and accordingly select the best option.*

19. Hearing the speech of their leader, the crowd was in _____ state of Euphoria.
    a a   b an
    c the   d no article required

20. "Please lay _____ extra plate for dinner", Malti told her cook.
    a a   b an
    c the   d no article required

Directions for Q (21-22) *Fill in the blanks with the most appropriate determiner and accordingly select the best option.*

21. "_____ chocolate ice-cream is really delicious", remarked Charan to his mother.
    a These   b That   c This   d Those

22. The pilot of the plane put on _____ parachute before jumping off.
    a their   b my   c our   d his

Directions for Q (23-24) *Fill in the blanks with the most appropriate preposition and accordingly select the best option.*

23. I don't always agree _____ what my parents tell me.
    a at   b with   c to   d after

24. It is not good running away _____ your loved ones.
    a with   b to   c from   d of

25. *Punctuate the given sentence to make it meaningful and accordingly select the best option.*

    you must bring the following to the examination a pen a ruler a pencil an eraser and your hall ticket
    a You must bring the following to the examination; a pen, a ruler, a pencil, an eraser, and your hall ticket?
    b You must bring the following to the examination, a pen, a ruler, a pencil, an eraser, and your hall ticket.
    c You must bring the following to the examination; a pen, a ruler, a pencil, an eraser, and your hall ticket.
    d You must bring the following to the examination: a pen, a ruler, a pencil, an eraser and your hall ticket.

Directions for Q (26-27) *Fill in the blanks with the most appropriate conjunction and accordingly select the best option.*

26. She practiced well _____ she could win the match
    a such that   b so that
    c and   d as well as

27. _____ I had seen the red light, I would have stopped.
    a If   b When
    c As   d Though

Directions for Q (28-29) *A notice is given below with some parts missing, but substituted by rectangles with numbers 28 and 29. Identify the text which the numbers may be substituted by from the options given below.*

XYZ Public School, Delhi
NOTICE

| 29 |

16th November, 2012

All the Activity Council members are informed to attend a meeting tomorrow at 10:30 AM in the Biology lab. The meeting is called to discuss the activites for Christmas Day. You should come with your ideas and the estimated cost as well as the infrastructure required. For further details please contact the undersigned.

| 28 |

Class X
(*Activity Coordinator*)

---

28. a Yours sincerely
    b St Mary's Higher Secondary School
    c Class Monitor
    d Arvind Solanki

29. a Christmas Day Celebrations
    b St Xavier's High School
    c Important Meeting
    d Yours sincerely

30. *Fill in the blank with the correct tense of the verb given in brackets immediately after the blank and accordingly select the best option.*

    My mother .... (stay) in a rented house for three years.
    a have stayed
    b had staying
    c has been staying
    d staying

Answers

1. b	2. d	3. c	4. a	5. c	6. d	7. c	8. a	9. d	10. c
11. b	12. d	13. a	14. c	15. a	16. d	17. b	18. a	19. a	20. b
21. c	22. d	23. b	24. c	25. d	26. b	27. a	28. d	29. a	30. c

Practice Set ②

A Whole Content Based Test for Class 8th English Olympiad

Directions for Q (1-5) *Read the passage carefully and select the option that you consider the most appropriate answer to each question.*

The History of Ice-Cream

George Washington went into debt over it, Nero sent slaves across his empire due to it and the success of modern day cafès owes a huge debt to it.

It is, of course, ice-cream. The Chinese are credited with being the first to add salt and saltpetre to snow or pounded ice to lower its freezing temperature in order to make frozen dairy dishes. Some experts claim that the process may have started during the Han Dynasty (206 BC - 220 AD), but food writers Weir and Liddell only present evidence from the Tang period (618 AD - 907 AD). However, the love of iced desserts and drinks dates back much further; the earliest ice-house (2250 BC) was unearthed in Iraq.

Nero loved his 'slushees' of snow flavoured with honey, fruit and wine. The Arab world had their 'charabs' and the Turks their 'chorbets'. Even Alexander the Great, after his conquest of Egypt in 332 BC, had 15 trenches dug and filled with snow for his cooled 'punches'!

The 1660s saw water ices in Spain and Italy as well as in the cities of Vienna and Paris, while Venice had its iced creams. However, it took the birth of the cafe to make them a popular fashion. When a Sicilian named Procope opened Paris' first cafe in 1686, it was the sorbets and ice-creams that entranced Parisian society as much as the coffee. Within 100 years, iced desserts had captivated diners from the USA to London to Scandinavia.

In the 1850s, an editor of The Age newspaper in Melbourne, James Harrison, invented the ice-maker and the refrigerator, thus making ice more readily available throughout the year.

Questions

1. The main purpose of the text is to __________.
   - a compare differences in iced desserts between cultures
   - b document the process of making iced desserts
   - c recount the development of iced desserts
   - d explain the popularity of iced desserts

2. In the third paragraph, the writer uses quotation marks around the words 'slushees' and 'punches' to show that __________.
   - a he wants to emphasise them
   - b he is using sarcasm
   - c they are modern terms
   - d they are taken from another text

3. According to the passage, the earliest discovered evidence for the consumption of iced desserts and drinks dates back to __________.
   - a 2250 BC
   - b 322 BC
   - c 206 BC - 220 AD
   - d 618 AD - 907 AD

4. Due to James Harrison's inventions __________.
   - a iced desserts became readily available in Melbourne
   - b iced desserts could be made throughout the year
   - c a wider range of ice-cream flavours could be created
   - d paper cups or dishes were not needed to serve ice-cream

5. In the fourth paragraph the word 'captivated' is nearest in meaning to __________.
   - a apprehended
   - b enthralled
   - c captured
   - d arrested

6. *Find the antonym of the word underlined in the sentence below and accordingly select the best option.*

   Sunil admitted his mistake in cheating during the final exams.
   - a abandoned
   - b repulsed
   - c challenged
   - d denied

7. *Change the sentence given below into direct speech and accordingly select the best option.*

My friend asked me when I usually got up.

   a My friend asked me, "When you usually got up?"

   b My friend said to me, "When do you usually got up?"

   c My friend said to me, "When do you usually get up?"

   d My friend questioned me, "When do you get up, usually?"

8. *Change the sentence given below to active voice and accordingly select the best option.*

The instructions were being read out by the supervisor.

   a The supervisor is reading out the instructions.

   b The supervisor was reading out the instructions.

   c The supervisor had been reading out the instructions.

   d The supervisor will reading out the instructions.

Directions for Q (9-10) *Fill in the blanks using appropriate tense forms and accordingly select the best option.*

9. We _______ the old man to the hospital last evening.

   a took   b take

   c have taken   d had taken

10. The doctor who treats him _______ that he _______ tomorrow.

   a said, will be discharged

   b says, would be discharged

   c has said, would be discharged

   d says, will be discharged

Directions for Q (11-13) *Fill in the blanks using appropriate articles or determiners and accordingly select the best option.*

11. We met _______ nice European girls on holiday.

   a an   b the

   c some   d any

12. I prefer _______ mountains to the seaside.

   a a   b the

   c some   d many

13. _______ umbrella is of no use in _______ thunderstorm.

   a An, a   b The, a

   c Many, a   d An, the

14. *In the passage below, the first and last sentences are identified as A and Z. The remaining four sentences are labelled as P, Q, R and S. Find the correct sequence of these four sentences and select the correct option accordingly.*

A Abraham Lincoln managed a shop for a few months during his youth.

P Lincoln would jump up, attend to the customer's needs and then go back to his reading.

Q Sometimes a chance customer would come to his shop.

R He used to lie full length on the counter of the shop reading a book.

S Abraham's method of running the shop was totally different from others.

Z Never before or after had young Abraham got so much time for reading as he had in those days.

   a PQRS   b RPSQ

   c SRQP   d RSQP

Directions for Q (15-16) *Select the option having the meaning nearest to the idioms underlined in the given sentences.*

15. Why don't you make a simple website for your business? <u>There's nothing to it.</u>

   a It's like eating cake

   b It doesn't require any money

   c It's very easy

   d It's not impossible

16. At the start of the meeting, Saurabh tried to <u>break the ice</u> by cracking a joke.

   a cool frayed tempers

   b sway opinion

   c entertain the opposite side

   d initiate interaction

Directions for Q (17-18) *Identify the grammatically incorrect sentence from the given options.*

17. a Last year I visited Australia for the first time.

      b The Mathematics teacher punished the boy because he hadn't made his homework.

      c Ramesh was in a hurry, so we couldn't talk to me.

      d Devinder fell off the ladder and fractured his leg.

18.   **a**   I went to Mussoorie for a holiday.

       b   I have cleaned the entire house except for the bathroom.

       c   Take the second turning on the left to reach the bus stand.

       d   The Delhi Vidhan Sabha consisting of seventy members.

Directions for Q (19-20) *Change the complex sentence given below into a compound sentence and accordingly select the best option.*

19. Besides making himself miserable, he makes others unhappy.

       a   Despite making others unhappy, he makes himself miserable.

       b   He makes others and himself miserable and unhappy.

       c   He makes others as well as himself miserable.

       d   He makes people beside himself miserable.

20. The problem was too difficult to be solved.

       a   The problem was very difficult and therefore we couldn't solve it.

       b   It was impossible to solve the problem.

       c   Because the problem was too difficult, it could not be solved.

       d   The problem was impossible for solution.

Directions for Q (21-22) *Punctuate the given sentence to make it meaningful and accordingly select the best option*

21. do you know if shes eligible and if she is eligible can she start the job tomorrow

       a   Do you know if she's eligible, and if she is eligible can she start the job tomorrow?

       b   Do you know if she's eligible and, if she is eligible, can she start the job tomorrow?

       c   Do you know if she's eligible, and if she is eligible can she start the job tomorrow.

       d   Do you know if she's eligible and if she is eligible, can she start the job tomorrow?

22. i am going Rizwan said to ask you a difficult question but you don't have to answer it

       a   "I am going," Rizwan said, "to ask you a difficult question, but don't you have to answer it?"

       b   "I am" going, Rizwan said, "to ask you a difficult question, but don't you have to answer it?"

       c   "I am going," Rizwan said, "to ask you a difficult question but you don't have to answer it?"

       d   "I am going," Rizwan said, "to ask you a difficult question, but you don't have to answer it."

Directions for Q (23-24) *A formal letter is given below with some parts missing, but substituted by rectangles with numbers 23 and 24. Identify the text which the numbers may be substituted by from the options given below.*

Customer Service Department
Saurabh Educational Publishers

> 23

11th April 20XX

Mr Girish Khurana
741, MG Road, Hapur - 245101

    Subject: Books Received in Damaged Condition

Dear Mr Khurana
Thank you for your letter dated 7th April 20XX regarding books sent by us through courier being received in damaged condition by you. We have contacted the courier agency responsible regarding this problem and will get back to you shortly. We cannot accept any blame in the matter, as we had packed the books securely.

We regret the inconvenience caused.

> 24

Despatch Officer

23.   **a**   A well-known publisher

       b   45 Sarvodaya Nagar, Meerut -250001

       c   First floor, Convenience Mall

       d   c/o Educational Courier Service

24.   **a**   With love

       b   Hope to see you soon

       c   Yours sincerely

       d   Saurabh Educational Publishers

25. *Find the option which is different from the others in any respect in the four given options. This means that one of the four given options does not belong to the group of the other three.*

     a Cub   **b** Bitch

     c Dog   **d** Puppy

26. *Fill in the blank with the most appropriate conjunction and accordingly select the best option.*

Other planets have small moons __________ ours is very large compared to the earth.

     a and

     b that

     c but

     d as well as

Practice Set 2

27. Rupesh had really no excuse _________ attacking that press photographer.

    a in   b of
    c from   d for

28. The young Major Jarnail Singh was entrusted _________ the task of suppressing the riots.

    a for   b with
    c to   d onto

29. You _________ for me. I could have reached there on my own.

    a couldn't wait   b didn't need to wait
    c neednt have waited d need not wait

30. I don't think that I _________ be able to come.

    a will   b would
    c can   d can't

Answers

1. c	2. d	3. a	4. b	5. b	6. d	7. c	8. b	9. a	10. d
11. c	12. b	13. a	14. c	15. c	16. d	17. b	18. d	19. c	20. a
21. b	22. d	23. b	24. c	25. a	26. c	27. d	28. b	29. c	30. a

Practice Set 2

Practice Set ③

A Whole Content Based Test for Class 8th English Olympiad

Directions for Q (1-5) *Read the passage carefully and select the option that you consider the most appropriate answer to each question.*

Children's playgrounds were at one time exciting places with 'flying foxes' to test their balance, 'monkey bars' from which they could hang precariously while viewing the world upside down and roundabouts that promised mild but thrilling bouts of nausea. Now they are bland places rarely visited by children. This has come about because municipalities are afraid that a child may fall and stub a toe, causing an angry parent to file a lawsuit claiming that the equipment is unsafe.

Recently two teenaged American girls sued a fast food company, claiming that the company was to blame for their obesity. Fortunately common sense prevailed and the case was dismissed. Given the amount of government publicity on the potential dangers of a fast food diet, surely teenagers know that an excessive intake of fats and sugars will result in weight gain. While advertising may be seductive and may present the food in enticing ways, it is the individual who makes the decision to approach the shop, purchase the food and eat it. No one forced these girls to eat these foods.

A culture of blame seems to permeate so many areas of our lives. It goes by many names. A 14-year old boy caught stealing a pair of jeans from a department store claimed that it was not really his fault. His friends made him do it, as they would not accept him as part of their group unless he complied. "Peer pressure is the real problem," explained his lawyer to the magistrate. "He was forced to steal to be accepted. Besides, the store had placed the rack of jeans outside the doorway, so some responsibility also lies with them. They should not have placed temptation in his way." Are we to believe that 14-year olds are unable to differentiate between right and wrong?

Parent lobby groups are calling for a ban on advertising of snack foods during children's TV programmes. They claim that they are powerless to resist their children's demands for these products. They call it 'pester power'. Whatever happened to saying "No" loudly and firmly? Even better, turn off the TV and send the children out to play. But first check the backyard. Have you put away that garden rake? Is the dog tied up? Have you removed any weak branches from the tree that they could possibly climb onto? Imagine the situation if they decided to sue you for any cuts or bruises resulting from a little healthy play!

Perhaps what we all need is a dose of 'person power': the power to accept personal responsibility for our actions.

Questions

1. According to the writer, the difference between children's playgrounds of the past and present is ______.

   a   municipalities now work with parents to prevent accidents on these playgrounds

   b   the playing equipment has become old-fashioned

   c   parents don't allow their children to play there any more

   d   the playing equipment no longer interests children

2. Which phrase from the first paragraph tells us that the writer thinks the municipalities have overreacted?

   a   file a lawsuit

   b   bouts of nausea

   c   causing an angry parent

   d   a child may fall and stub a toe

3. The writer has little sympathy for the teenaged girls because she feels that ______.

   a   by suing the fast food companies, the girls are being dishonest

   b   the girls were already obese from eating other types of fast food

   c   sufficient information is available to tell that a fast food diet can lead to obesity

   d   fast food companies already receive too much negative media publicity

4. What was the main argument that the lawyer made to defend the boy who stole a pair of jeans?

   a The boy was enticed into stealing the jeans because no one was watching the clothing rack.

   b The boy did not know that stealing the jeans was a criminal offence.

   c The boy's friends were undesirable characters who misled the boy.

   d The boy's decision to steal the jeans was influenced by wanting to comply with his friends' wishes.

5. The term 'pester power' is best understood as ______.

   a the increasing importance of children in the family

   b the lack of resistance shown by parents to their children's demands

   c the ability of children to manipulate their parents

   d the loss of discipline among children

Directions for Q (6 -7) *Fill in the blanks using suitable connectors and accordingly select the best option.*

6. Childhood is the period of life ________ the seeds of character are sown.

   a in   b where
   c if   d when

7. Passengers are warned ________ it is dangerous to lean out of the window ________ the train is in motion.

   a if, after   b that, otherwise
   c that, when   d on, when

Directions for Q (8-9) *Fill in the blanks with the correct tense of the verbs given in brackets immediately after the blanks and accordingly select the best option.*

8. Irfan ________ (undergo) treatment for the past one year for his tumour.

   a has been undergoing
   b is been undergoing
   c has already undergone
   d has underwent

9. The doctor who treats Satyendra ________ (say) that he ________ (discharge) tomorrow from the nursing home.

   a said, will be discharged
   b has said, would be discharged
   c says, would be discharged
   d says, will be discharged

Directions for Q (10-11) *The sentence given below contains an underlined word and a blank space. You have to fill in the blank using a word that is an antonym of the underlined word, and select the best option accordingly.*

10. Praveen showed no <u>sympathy</u> towards the poor, as his attitude was full of ________.

    a apathy   b hostility
    c unresponsive   d enthusiasm

11. Mr Chawla became a <u>spendthrift</u> in his old age, but when he was young he was a ________.

    a profligate   b waster
    c miser   d spender

Directions for Q (12-13) *Change the sentence given to passive voice so that it expresses the same idea and accordingly select the best option.*

12. The History teacher punished the students who had not done their homework.

    a The students who had not done their homework punished by the History teacher.

    b The students who had not done their homework had been punished by the History teacher.

    c The students who had not done their homework were punished by the History teacher.

    d The students who did not do their homework were being punished by the History teacher.

13. Our pet cat has drunk all the milk.

    a All the milk has been drunk by our pet cat.
    b All the milk is drunk by our pet, the cat.
    c All the milk had been drunk by the pet cat.
    d All the milk is being drunk by our pet cat.

Directions for Q (14-15) *Change the sentence given below into direct speech and accordingly select the best option.*

14. Ravinder asked me if I could solve that problem.

    a I asked Ravinder, "Can you solve this problem?"

    b "Can you solve this problem?", Ravinder asked me.

    c I asked Ravinder, "Could you solve this problem?"

    d "Could you solve this problem?", Ravinder asked me.

Practice Set 3

15. Ulysses asked the little bird whether it had anything to tell him.

   a "Can you tell me something, little bird?" asked Ulysses.

   b Ulysses asked the little bird, "What do you have to tell me?"

   c Ulysses asked, "Little bird, have you something to tell me?"

   d "Have you anything to tell me, little bird?" asked Ulysses.

Directions for Q (16-17) *Change the sentence given below into a simple sentence and accordingly select the best option.*

16. As the weather was rough, the sailors cancelled the voyage across the channel.

   a The sailors cancelled the voyage across the channel because the weather was rough.

   b The weather being rough, the sailors cancelled the voyage across the channel.

   c The sailors cancelled the voyage across the channel because of the weather being rough.

   d The weather was rough and so the sailors cancelled the voyage across the channel.

17. Although Beena worked very hard, she failed her exam.

   a Beena failed the exam in spite of working very hard.

   b Beena failed the exam although she worked very hard.

   c Beena failed the exam despite of working very hard.

   d Although Beena failed the exam, but she had worked very hard.

18. *In the passage below, the first and last sentences are identified as A and Z. The remaining four sentences are labelled as P, Q, R and S. Find the correct sequence of these four sentences and select the correct option accordingly.*

   A The tribal settlement is called 'Podu'.

   P The huts have entrances as low as three to four feet.

   Q It is located in a safe place, sheltered from wild animals.

   R Bamboo is used along with sticks and twigs to make the walls, which are then plastered with mud to a height of about three feet.

   S It usually consists of a group of ten to fifty huts.

   Z The roof is made of bamboo mesh, dried grass and tree bark.

   a PQRS

   b QPSR

   c SPQR

   d QSPR

19. *Find the option which is different from the others in any respect in the four options given. This means that one of the four options given does not belong to the group of the other three.*

   a Cock   b Drake

   c Doe   d Bull

20. *Select the option having the meaning nearest to the idiom underlined in the given sentence.*

   Damayanti <u>crossed her fingers</u>, wishing it would not rain on her wedding day.

   a prayed

   b hoped for good luck

   c became cheerful

   d daydreamed

Directions for Q (21-22) *Identify the grammatically correct sentence from the given options*

21.
   a Harleen met Mohit on the first time last month.

   b Although the money was missing, Sarita had not take it.

   c Lata is good at playing instruments as the guitar.

   d Please don't use your nail as a screwdriver.

22.
   a You may cultivate your hobbies as long as they do not interfere with your studies.

   b Kailash has being informed of the gravity of the situation.

   c I was indignant at the way Ashok was treated his servants.

   d Vishwas has been hostile against me right from the beginning.

Directions for Q (23-24) *Fill in the blanks with the most appropriate modal and accordingly select the best option.*

23. I was worried that if I asked him again, he ________ refuse.

   a should   b might

   c can   d may

24. If you ________ see him, give him my regards.

   a will   b would

   c should   d shall

Practice Set 3

To: sara1234@gmail.com

Cc: 25

Subject: Important Email

Dear Sir,
Action is being taken on your complaint. Kindly bear with us till the next mail message you receive from us.
With regards

26

25.
  a Sarvesh Ahuja
  b Marketing Manager
  c kalia234@gmail.com
  d pravesh*4321

26.
  a See you soon
  b Thanking you
  c Saurabh Educational Publishers
  d Sarvesh Ahuja, Service Department

27. *Punctuate the given sentence to make it meaningful and accordingly select the best option.*

when the teacher commented that her spelling was poor karuna replied all the members of my family are poor spellers why not me

  a When the teacher commented that her spelling was poor, Karuna replied, "All the members of my family are poor spellers. Why not me?"
  b When the teacher commented, that her spelling was poor Karuna replied "all the members of my family are poor spellers. Why not me?"
  c When the teacher commented that her spelling was poor Karuna replied that all the members of her family are poor spellers. Why not me?
  d When the teacher commented that her spelling was poor Karuna replied "all the members of my family are poor spellers. Why not me?"

Directions for Q (28-29) *Fill in the blanks using appropriate articles or determiners and accordingly select the best option.*

28. Talib Hussain said that _________ safest place in India was _________ Sleeper compartment in _________ express train.
  a a, the, a   b the, the, an
  c the, some, any   d any, the, an

29. It is _________ responsibility of _________ government to protect _________ private property.
  a the, the, (no article / determiner)
  b the, any, some
  c (no article / determiner), the, any
  d a, the, any

30. *Fill in the blanks with the most appropriate conjunctions and accordingly select the best option.*
Sujata ______ phoned ______ wrote any message after she left home.
  a either, or   b while, and
  c though, or   d neither, nor

Answers

1. d	2. a	3. c	4. d	5. b	6. d	7. c	8. a	9. d	10. b
11. c	12. c	13. a	14. b	15. d	16. b	17. a	18. d	19. c	20. b
21. d	22. a	23. b	24. c	25. c	26. d	27. a	28. b	29. a	30. d

Practice Set 3

Answer & Explanations

1   *Active and Passive Voice*

Exercise I
1. (b)   2. (a)   3. (a)   4. (a)   5. (c)   6. (a)   7. (b)   8. (c)   9. (a)   10. (b)

Exercise II
1. (b)   2. (b)   3. (b)   4. (b)   5. (a)   6. (c)   7. (b)   8. (c)   9. (c)   10. (a)

Exercise III
1. (c)   2. (b)   3. (c)   4. (a)   5. (b)   6. (a)   7. (b)   8. (b)   9. (a)   10. (b)
11. (c)

Exercise IV
1. (a)   2. (b)   3. (c)   4. (c)   5. (a)   6. (b)   7. (a)   8. (c)   9. (a)   10. (c)

Exercise V
1. (b)   2. (b)   3. (c)   4. (a)   5. (a)

2   *Punctuation*

Exercise I
1. (b)   2. (a)   3. (c)   4. (a)   5. (b)   6. (b)   7. (c)   8. (c)

Exercise II
1. (a)   2. (c)   3. (b)   4. (c)   5. (a)   6. (c)   7. (c)

Exercise III
1. (a)   2. (b)   3. (c)   4. (b)   5. (c)   6. (b)

Exercise IV
1. (b)   2. (c)   3. (a)   4. (b)   5. (c)   6. (b)   7. (a)   8. (c)   9. (c)   10. (b)

Exercise V
(Capitalisation and punctuation marks are shown in **bold**)

Sharks **-** known to mariners as **"**sea dogs**",** are a group of fish characterised by a cartilaginous skeleton, five to seven gill slits on the sides of the head, and pectoral fins which are not fused to the head. **W**ell-known species such as the great white shark, tiger shark, blue shark, and the hammerhead shark are apex predators. **E**ven though their survival is threatened by human-related activities**;** they are organisms at the top of their underwater food chain. **T**heir predatory skill fascinates and frightens humans. **A** shark's teeth are embedded in its gums rather than its jaw. **T**hey are constantly replaced throughout the shark's life. **M**ultiple rows of replacement teeth grow in a groove on the inside of the jaw and steadily move forward in comparison to a conveyor belt. **S**ome sharks lose 30000 or more teeth in their lifetime.

Exercise VI
(Capitalisation and punctuation marks are shown in **bold**)

A large number of today's children do not know who **B**etty **C**rocker is. **"T**here're a lot of people who used to rely on her cookbooks**,"** says my mother.

True**!** Back in the 1930s, Betty Crocker was a name everyone knew. However, the name **"**Betty Crocker**"** actually came from an employee's imagination. Marjorie Husted said in 1930, **"W**e'll make her look like the average American homemaker.**"**

Betty Crocker's **"**101 Delicious Bisquick Creations**"** was the name of one of her books. **A**nd a television commercial asked**,** **"W**ho's the person whose cookies we love?**" S**oon boxes of Betty's cake, brownie and biscuit mixes appeared on the shelves of supermarkets.

In 1946, Betty **C**rocker was voted the United States' second most popular woman. (Eleanor Roosevelt was first). **F**ew people realised that she didn't really exist. **S**he was simply General Mills' icon. **A**s women's fashions changed, the company updated her picture. **H**er appearance became more professional looking as women entered the business world. **P**eople agreed with the commercial that told them, **"B**uy Betty Crocker. **I**t's a quality you can trust.**"**

In honour of this fictitious woman, a street was named after her. **T**he street's name is **B**etty **C**rocker **D**rive.

3 Prepositions

Exercise I

1. (b)	2. (d)	3. (c)	4. (a)	5. (d)	6. (a)	7. (d)	8. (c)	9. (d)	10. (a)

Exercise II

1. (c)	2. (b)	3. (d)	4. (d)	5. (d)	6. (b)	7. (c)	8. (c)	9. (d)	10. (b)

Exercise III

1. (b)	2. (a)	3. (d)	4. (c)	5. (b)	6. (b)	7. (c)	8. (b)	9. (d)	10. (a)

Exercise IV

1. (c)	2. (b)	3. (b)	4. (c)	5. (a)	6. (b)	7. (b)	8. (c)	9. (b)	10. (a)

Exercise V

1. (b)	2. (a)	3. (b)	4. (b)	5. (b)	6. (c)	7. (b)	8. (a)	9. (a)	10. (a)

Exercise VI

1. (a)	2. (c)	3. (d)	4. (b)	5. (a)	6. (c)	7. (b)	8. (a)	9. (c)	10. (d)
11. (c)	12. (d)	13. (b)	14. (a)	15. (d)	16. (b)	17. (c)	18. (d)	19. (a)	20. (b)
21. (a)	22. (c)	23. (b)	24. (c)	25. (d)					

4 Determiners

Exercise I

1. (a)	2. (c)	3. (d)	4. (a)	5. (b)	6. (c)	7. (b)	8. (b)	9. (a)	10. (b)

Exercise II

1. (a)	2. (b)	3. (b)	4. (b)	5. (a)	6. (a)	7. (b)	8. (a)	9. (a)	10. (b)

Exercise III

1. (b)	2. (a)	3. (b)	4. (b)	5. (c)	6. (b)	7. (b)	8. (b)	9. (b)	10. (a)
11. (c)	12. (c)	13. (c)	14. (b)	15. (c)	16. (a)	17. (a)	18. (c)	19. (b)	20. (a)
21. (b)	22. (b)	23. (c)	24. (c)	25. (b)					

Exercise IV

1. (d)	2. (a)	3. (c)	4. (a)	5. (c)	6. (c)	7. (c)	8. (d)	9. (a)	10. (b)

Exercise V

1. (c)	2. (a)	3. (c) or (a)	4. (c)	5. (a)	6. (a)	7. (a)	8. (a) or (c)	9. (c)	10. (a)
11. (a)	12. (a)	13. (a)	14. (a)	15. (b)	16. (d)	17. (a)			

5 Verb Tenses

Exercise I

1. (b)	2. (b)	3. (a)	4. (a)	5. (b)	6. (c)	7. (b)	8. (a)	9. (b)	10. (a)
11. (c)	12. (a)	13. (a)	14. (b)	15. (b)	16. (b)	17. (a)	18. (b)	19. (a)	20. (a)
21. (b)	22. (c)	23. (a)	24. (b)	25. (a)					

Exercise II

1. (b)	2. (b)	3. (a)	4. (c)	5. (c)	6. (a)	7. (a)	8. (b)	9. (a)	10. (a)
11. (c)	12. (a)	13. (a)	14. (a)	15. (b)	16. (c)	17. (a)	18. (a)	19. (b)	

Exercise III

1. (b)	2. (a)	3. (c)	4. (b)	5. (d)	6. (a)	7. (c)	8. (a)	9. (a)	10. (b)
11. (b)	12. (a)	13. (a)	14. (b)	15. (c)	16. (b)	17. (b)	18. (a)		

Exercise IV

1. (a)	2. (b)	3. (c)	4. (b)	5. (d)	6. (b)	7. (a)	8. (d)	9. (c)	10. (a)
11. (a)	12. (c)	13. (c)	14. (c)	15. (d)	16. (a)	17. (b)	18. (b)	19. (b)	20. (c)
21. (d)	22. (a)	23. (c)	24. (b)	25. (a)					

ENGLISH **OLYMPIAD** CLASS VIII

6 Word Meaning in Context

1. (d)	2. (a)	3. (c)	4. (b)	5. (c)	6. (b)	7. (a)	8. (b)	9. (c)	10. (a)
11. (c)	12. (d)	13. (b)	14. (c)	15. (a)	16. (d)	17. (d)	18. (b)	19. (a)	20. (c)

7 Error Detection

Exercise I

1. A	2. A	3. A	4. B	5. C	6. A	7. B	8. B	9. D	10. E
11. D	12. B	13. D	14. C	15. C	16. C	17. A	18. B	19. B	20. C

Exercise II

1. D	2. D	3. B	4. D	5. D	6. C	7. C	8. C	9. B	10. C
11. D	12. C								

8 Connectors

Exercise I

1. (b)	2. (a)	3. (c)	4. (a)	5. (a)	6. (c)	7. (b)	8. (a)	9. (c)	10. (a)

Exercise II

1. (c)	2. (b)	3. (d)	4. (a)	5. (c)	6. (b)	7. (d)	8. (d)	9. (a)	10. (b)

Exercise III

1. (a)	2. (b)	3. (c)	4. (d)	5. (c)	6. (d)	7. (a)	8. (a)	9. (a)	10. (b)

Exercise IV

1. (b)	2. (b)	3. (a)	4. (b)	5. (b)	6. (a)	7. (a)	8. (a)	9. (a)	10. (a)

Exercise V

1. (a)	2. (b)	3. (b)	4. (d)	5. (c)	6. (b)	7. (b)	8. (d)	9. (a)	10. (c)

Exercise VI

1. (b)	2. (d)	3. (a)	4. (d)	5. (d)	6. (d)	7. (b)	8. (a)	9. (d)	10. (a)

9 Logical Sequencing

Logical Sequencing in an Action

1. (d)	2. (b)	3. (c)	4. (d)	5. (a)	6. (b)	7. (a)	8. (d)	9. (c)	10. (b)

Logical Sequencing in a Process

1. (d)	2. (b)	3. (c)	4. (c)	5. (a)

Logical Sequencing in a Story

1. (d)	2. (a)	3. (c)	4. (d)	5. (b)

Jumbled Sentence

1. (c)	2. (b)	3. (a)	4. (d)	5. (d)	6. (d)	7. (b)	8. (c)	9. (c)	10. (a)
11. (d)	12. (b)	13. (c)	14. (c)	15. (a)	16. (a)	17. (d)	18. (d)	19. (b)	20. (c)

10 Transformation of Sentences

Exercise I

1. (a)	2. (b)	3. (a)	4. (b)	5. (b)	6. (a)	7. (c)	8. (a)	9. (a)	10. (b)

Exercise II

1. (a)	2. (b)	3. (a)	4. (c)	5. (b)	6. (a)	7. (b)	8. (b)	9. (a)	10. (b)

Exercise III

| 1. (b) | 2. (a) | 3. (a) | 4. (b) | 5. (a) | 6. (a) | 7. (b) | 8. (b) | 9. (a) | 10. (b) |

Exercise IV

| 1. (b) | 2. (b) | 3. (b) | 4. (a) | 5. (a) | 6. (b) | 7. (a) | 8. (a) | 9. (b) | 10. (b) |

Exercise V

| 1. (b) | 2. (b) | 3. (a) | 4. (c) | 5. (a) | 6. (b) | 7. (c) | 8. (c) | 9. (a) | 10. (b) |

Exercise VI

| 1. (c) | 2. (b) | 3. (c) | 4. (a) | 5. (b) | 6. (a) | 7. (b) | 8. (b) | 9. (b) | 10. (b) |

Exercise VII

| 1. (b) | 2. (c) | 3. (b) | 4. (a) | 5. (b) | 6. (a) | 7. (b) | 8. (b) | 9. (a) | 10. (b) |

Exercise VIII

| 1. (a) | 2. (b) | 3. (c) | 4. (b) | 5. (b) | 6. (c) | 7. (b) | 8. (c) |

Exercise IX

| 1. (a) | 2. (b) | 3. (b) | 4. (c) | 5. (a) | 6. (b) | 7. (a) | 8. (b) |

Exercise X

| 1. (b) | 2. (a) | 3. (a) | 4. (c) | 5. (c) | 6. (a) | 7. (c) | 8. (b) | 9. (a) | 10. (c) |
| 11. (a) | 12. (b) |

11 Direct and Reported Speech

Exercise I

| 1. (c) | 2. (b) | 3. (c) | 4. (b) | 5. (a) | 6. (b) | 7. (b) | 8. (a) | 9. (b) | 10. (a) |

Exercise II

| 1. (b) | 2. (c) | 3. (a) | 4. (b) | 5. (b) | 6. (c) | 7. (c) | 8. (d) | 9. (b) | 10. (a) |

Exercise III

| 1. (b) | 2. (b) | 3. (a) | 4. (a) | 5. (a) | 6. (b) | 7. (a) | 8. (c) | 9. (c) | 10. (a) |

Exercise IV

| 1. (a) | 2. (c) | 3. (b) | 4. (c) | 5. (b) | 6. (c) | 7. (a) | 8. (b) | 9. (b) | 10. (a) |
| 11. (a) | 12. (a) | 13. (c) | 14. (a) |

Exercise V

| 1. (a) | 2. (c) | 3. (a) | 4. (a) | 5. (b) |

12 Cloze Test

Exercise I

| 1. (d) | 2. (a) | 3. (b) | 4. (b) | 5. (c) | 6. (d) | 7. (a) | 8. (a) | 9. (c) | 10. (c) |
| 11. (d) | 12. (b) | 13. (b) | 14. (d) | 15. (a) |

Exercise II

| 1. (d) | 2. (b) | 3. (a) | 4. (c) | 5. (b) | 6. (d) | 7. (a) | 8. (c) | 9. (c) | 10. (a) |

Exercise III

| 1. (a) | 2. (b) | 3. (c) | 4. (d) | 5. (c) | 6. (a) | 7. (b) | 8. (d) | 9. (a) | 10. (b) |
| 11. (a) | 12. (d) | 13. (d) | 14. (a) | 15. (a) | 16. (d) | 17. (c) | 18. (b) | 19. (a) | 20. (d) |

ENGLISH **OLYMPIAD** CLASS VIII

Exercise I

| 1. (b) | 2. (c) | 3. (c) | 4. (a) | 5. (b) | 6. (a) | 7. (b) | 8. (b) | 9. (b) | 10. (a) |

Exercise II

| 1. (c) | 2. (b) | 3. (c) | 4. (b) | 5. (c) | 6. (a) | 7. (b) | 8. (a) | 9. (d) | 10. (b) |

Exercise III

| 1. (b) | 2. (c) | 3. (c) | 4. (b) | 5. (c) | 6. (b) | 7. (c) | 8. (c) | 9. (c) | 10. (b) |

Exercise IV

| 1. (c) | 2. (a) | 3. (b) | 4. (a) | 5. (a) | 6. (a) | 7. (b) | 8. (a) | 9. (b) | 10. (a) |

Exercise V

| 1. (b) | 2. (a) | 3. (d) | 4. (c) | 5. (b) | 6. (d) | 7. (c) | 8. (a) | 9. (c) | 10. (d) |

14 *Reading Comprehension*

Passage I

1. **(a)** This question tests our understanding of a definition. Only the sugar maple (in the first sentence) is defined. The options (b), (c) and (d), even though mentioned in the passage, are not defined.

2. **(b)** This is a specific detail question. Based on the information in the passage, sapping takes place at the end of the winter and in early spring. Therefore, (b) is the best answer.

3. **(d)** This question tests our inference ability. The answer to the question is not directly stated in the passage. Option (d) is the best answer. The production technique is quite straightforward, but it takes time. The producers have to depend on the natural flow of the sap.

4. **(d)** This is a language expression question. The correct answer is based on the antecedent, the noun to which the pronoun refers. Reading the sentence, we notice that 'its' is a possessive pronoun which refers to the noun phrase, the sugar maple tree; therefore, (d) is the correct choice.

5. **(c)** This question tests our understanding of how the author organises the information in the passage. Most of the passage explains a step-by-step process of how maple syrup is made; thus, the correct option is (c). The author does not attempt to convince the reader; consequently, option (a) is not true. The passage neither expresses the causes of the maple syrup production nor lists the similarities between pure and commercial maple syrup; therefore, options (b) and (d) are incorrect.

Passage II

1. **(c)** This idiom can refer to a person or an object. Since the object referred to here is the pipeline, the correct option is (c). All the other options refer to a person.

2. **(b)** Based on what is given in the sentence, we can infer that (b) is the best answer. The other options do not fit into the context.

3. **(d)** The answer to the question is given in the phrase 'paid into the pipeline construction fund according to the size of its holdings' in the third sentence of the last paragraph. Thus, (d) is the correct answer. The other options are not mentioned in the passage.

4. **(c)** The author states the term 'permafrost' for an earth covering that always remains frozen. Options (a) and (b) mention 'frozen', but do not provide a term for an earth covering that always remains frozen. Option (d) is not relevant in this context.

5. **(d)** This question tests our understanding of the information given in the passage. Most of the passage explains about the construction of the pipeline; so the correct choice is (d). Cost of construction is mentioned, not the operating cost; thus option (a) is incorrect. Options (b) and (c) are not mentioned in the passage.

Passage III

1. **(c)** The first stanza mentions 'frosty night' and 'The year is dying', which confirms this option as correct.

2. **(d)** Happiness is mentioned throughout the poem as what is wanted by the poet.

3. **(a)** The last line mentions 'sweeter manners' to be rung in, so they are not to be rung out.

4. **(c)** The last two lines of the third stanza confirm this option as correct.

5. **(a)** The last two lines of the third stanza confirm this option as correct.

Passage IV

1. **(d)** The last sentence of the second paragraph confirms this option as correct. Options (a), (b) and (c) are not related to converting the country into a barren wasteland.

2. **(c)** The word 'beyond' means 'more than' or 'further'. Thus this option is correct. Option (a) states just the reverse. Option (b) is not mentioned in the passage. Option (d) is not having the sense of belief.

3. **(a)** Whatever has been mentioned in the fourth paragraph before this phrase gives a very bleak picture of the future of Nauruans. Thus this option is correct. Option (b) states just the reverse, thus being incorrect. Options (c) and (d) are not mentioned in the paragraph.

4. **(c)** The second, third and fourth paragraphs bring out this option as the correct answer. Options (a) and (d) are mentioned in the paragraph, but not in relation to being unfortunate. Option (b) is not mentioned at all.

5. **(b)** 'Recklessly' means 'lacking care about the consequences'. Thus option (b) is the correct antonym.

   Options (a) and (c) are synonyms, not antonyms, of 'recklessly'. Option (d) means, 'more than what one can afford', thus not being an antonym.

Passage V

1. **(d)** This idiom means 'to make good use of opportunities while they last'. Option (a) and (c) refer literally to hay and the sun, thus being incorrect. Option (b) is irrelevant.

2. **(b)** Option (b) is mentioned in the sixth sentence of the first paragraph. Options (a) and (c) are not mentioned in the context of taking loans.

3. **(b)** The fourth sentence of the first paragraph confirms this option as correct.

   Option (a) states just the condition of the farmer without giving the reason. Options (c) and (d) are not relevant.

4. **(a)** The fifth sentence of the first paragraph brings out this option as the correct answer.

   Options (b) and (c) are not mentioned in the paragraph.

5. **(c)** The word 'abject' means, 'without any pride or respect for yourself'. Thus the word 'proud' is the correct antonym.

   Options (a) and (b) are synonyms for 'abject', whereas option (d) is not related.

Passage VI

1. **(c)** The second line of the first and second stanzas and the third line of the third stanza bring out this option as the correct one.

2. **(a)** The other options all imply something sad, whereas the poem is the reverse of this.

3. **(c)** Compassion of the poet towards the reader is highlighted in each of the stanzas.

4. **(d)** This is the only option which matches the context (third line of the second stanza).

5. **(b)** The last line of the poem mentions 'love', which means the same as 'affection' in the context.

Passage VII

1. **(c)** In the second paragraph, Simon is mentioned as reluctant to enter the office of the Agency. Also, during the conversation with the salesman, he hesitates and also wriggles uncomfortably.

All this shows that he is feeling awkward. The other three options are not brought out in the passage.

2. **(a)** What Simon says in the sixth paragraph confirms this option as correct. The other three options are not brought out in the passage.

3. **(b)** The meaning of 'squeamish' is 'easily upset by unpleasant sights'. Also, the 'Sacking of Carthage' was involving much shedding of blood, which would be an unpleasant sight for anyone to see.

4. **(d)** The salesman is talking very smoothly and answering all of Simon's queries, which shows that he is confident and organised in his approach in selling tours into the past. Thus, the other options are invalid.

5. **(b)** The expression, 'with hands clasped before him' implies that he is being respectful to his prospective customer. The other three options do not match with the behaviour of the salesman during his conversation with Simon.

Passage VIII

1. **(c)** The end of the second paragraph and the start of the third paragraph tell us that the truck took them to the camp site, from where they went ahead by foot

   The other options are not brought out in the passage.

2. **(b)** The third sentence of the second paragraph confirms that this option is correct. The other three options are not mentioned or implied in the passage.

3. **(d)** The last phrase in this sentence is said in the form of a joke, as nobody would survive a fall from such a height. The other options cannot be concluded from the author's remarks.

4. **(c)** Only this option has two synonyms. The other options have words which mean different from each other.

5. **(a)** 'The quiet … was deafening' is an oxymoron, i.e. a phrase that combines two or more words that seem to be the opposite of each other.

   This implies that the quiet was significant or noticeable. The other three options do not match the context of the passage.

Passage IX

1. **(b)** The first sentence of the passage confirms this option as correct. The other options are not relevant in this context.

2. **(d)** The last sentence of the first paragraph means the same as this option. The other options are not mentioned in the passage.

3. **(c)** The second sentence of the second paragraph brings out the correctness of this option.

   Options (a), (b) and (d) are neither mentioned nor implied in the passage.

4. **(a)** This idiom means, 'to remain in power'. Thus this option is correct. The other options are not relevant in the context.

5. **(d)** The word 'honoured' here means 'respected' or 'obeyed'. The other options are not relevant to the context.

Passage X

1. **(d)** The first sentence of the passage confirms this option as correct. The other options are responsibilities of the police, as mentioned in different places in the passage.

2. **(c)** This option is a paraphrase of the first sentence. The other options are neither mentioned nor implied in the passage.

3. **(d)** Option (a) is implied by the fifth sentence of the second paragraph. Option (b) is implied by the fourth sentence of the second paragraph. Option (c) is implied by the last sentence of the first paragraph.

   Only option (d) is neither mentioned nor implied in the passage.

4. **(b)** Option (a) has a similar sense to the word, whereas options (c) and (d) are not relevant.

5. **(a)** Option (a) best paraphrases this statement. The other options are mentioned in the passage, but are not relevant here.

Passage XI

1. **(d)** This option states what the author is trying to convey - starting with priests, monks, and medicine men in medieval times, specialisation in the ninth century, as a compounder of medications in the 19th century, decline of compounding in the 1950s to the customised medications of today.

   Options (a), (b) and (c) are implied in the passage, but do not convey the message of the passage as a whole.

2. **(b)** The second sentence of the second paragraph mentions that commercial drug manufacturers were created in the 1950s and 1960s, not became abundant. Thus this option is correct.

   The other options are stated or implied at different places in the passage.

ENGLISH **OLYMPIAD** CLASS VIII

3. **(a)** This option is brought out as correct by the last sentence of the first paragraph.

The other options mention time periods when other changes occurred in the history of pharmacy.

4. **(c)** The word 'medications' in this sentence implies that they have been prescribed by an individual who makes informed medicinal decisions. Thus this option is correct.

Option (a) defines the role of a compounder. Option (b) is incorrect, as otherwise the doctor would not be able to prescribe a medication. Option (d) is not mentioned or implied in the passage.

5. **(b)** This option best suits the meaning being conveyed in this sentence. The other options are not relevant.

Passage XII

1. **(c)** The first and second line of the first stanza bring out this option as the correct one.

2. **(a)** The birds are asleep in their nests at night and so they do not have any thoughts.

3. **(b)** The last two lines of the third stanza and the first two lines of the fourth stanza bring out this option as the correct one.

4. **(d)** The moon is metaphorically termed as a flower in the bouquet of the heavens.

5. **(a)** The other options are not relevant in the context.

15 *Writing Skills*

Exercise I

A.1. (c)   2. (d)   3. (d)   4. (b)   5. (a)

B. (b)

C.1. (b)   2. (a)   3. (c)   4. (a)   5. (a)   6. (c)   7. (b)   8. (a)   9. (a)   10. (c)

11. (d)   12. (d)   13. (b)   14. (a)   15. (c)

D.1. (a)   2. (c)   3. (b)   4. (a)   5. (c)   6. (c)   7. (b)   8. (c)

Exercise II

A.1. (d)   2. (a)   3. (b)   4. (c)   5. (c)

B.1. (c)   2. (a)   3. (c)   4. (b)   5. (a)   6. (b)   7. (a)

Exercise III

A.1. (b)   2. (a)   3. (c)   4. (d)   5. (d)

B.6. (b)   7. (a)   8. (a)   9. (b)   10. (b)   11. (a)   12. (b)   13. (b)

C.1. (d)   2. (c)   3. (a)   4. (a)   5. (a)   6. (b)   7. (a)   8. (c)

www.ingramcontent.com/pod-product-compliance
Lightning Source LLC
LaVergne TN
LVHW080609200726
843509LV00007B/281